WITCHES, GHOSTS
AND SIGNS

WITCHES, GHOSTS AND SIGNS

Folklore of the Southern Appalachians

❖❖❖❖❖❖❖❖❖❖❖❖❖❖❖❖❖❖❖❖❖❖❖❖❖❖❖❖❖❖❖❖❖❖❖❖❖

Second Edition

PATRICK W. GAINER

WITH A PREFACE AND MOTIF INDEX BY

JUDY PROZZILLO BYERS

Director,

The Frank & Jane Gabor West Virginia Folklife Center,
Fairmont State University

MORGANTOWN 2008

West Virginia University Press, Morgantown 26506
© 2008 West Virginia University Press
All rights reserved.
First edition 1975 published by Seneca Books
Second edition 2008 with "Preface to the Second Edition" and "Appendix" by
Judy Prozzillo Byers, published by West Virginia University Press

15 14 13 12 11 10 09 08   8 7 6 5 4 3 2 1

ISBN 978-1-933202-20-4 [paperback]

Witches, ghosts, and signs: folklore of the Southern Appalachians
p. cm. —
1. Tales – West Virginia. 2. Ghosts – West Virginia. 3. Folklore – Appalachian
Mountains, Southern. I. Title. II. Gainer, Patrick Ward, 1904-1981. III. Byers,
Judy Prozzillo,
IN PROCESS

Library of Congress Control Number: 2008923588
Printed in U.S.A.

Contents

❖❖❖❖❖❖❖❖❖

Preface to the Second Edition

❖❖❖❖❖❖❖❖❖❖❖❖❖❖❖❖❖❖❖❖❖❖❖❖❖❖❖❖❖❖❖❖

Dr. Patrick Gainer was a legend to the decades of students who attended his folklore classes at West Virginia University's main campus in Morgantown, in extension throughout the state, and at Glenville State College. When I first met him, I was just a child and didn't know then that he was "bigger than real life." Dr. Ruth Ann Musick, my mentor, had brought me to a meeting of the West Virginia Folklore Society held at Fairmont State College. She was the archivist and editor for the society, and Gainer was the president, a position that he maintained until his death years later in 1981. As he stood on stage and introduced the program, in my childish viewpoint, I sized him up and recorded him unforgettable. He was not a giant; on the contrary, he was a jolly little man dressed in an oversized brown and gray tweed jacket with suede elbow patches. His tousled black hair, generously peppered with white, crowned his shiny face and twinkling eyes. When he spoke, his voice was slightly high-pitched, and his words rolled out like small bells tinkling. He had definitely caught my imagination.

Throughout my childhood, I met Gainer several more times when the West Virginia Folklore Society held meetings in Fairmont. Musick and Gainer were the sustaining leadership for this organization that had begun decades earlier by folklore enthusiasts at both West Virginia University (WVU) and Fairmont State College (FSC). In 1915, during a lecture series at West Virginia University's Summer School, Dr. C. Alphonso Smith of the University of Virginia encouraged the collection and preservation of English and Scottish popular ballads of the South. Heeding his call, the

West Virginia Folklore Society was founded in Morgantown on July 15, 1915, by three professors who became its first officers: Dr. John Harrington Cox of WVU, president, archivist, and general editor; Dr. Robert Allen Armstrong of WVU, vice president; and Dr. Walter Barnes of Fairmont State Normal School (later Fairmont State College), secretary-treasurer and official correspondent. At the society meetings, Gainer enjoyed hearing the ghost tales that Musick was collecting from my family, especially my grandmother. When I was a student at Fairmont State College, through Musick's influence, my interest in folklore blossomed. After my undergraduate days, she guided me to West Virginia University to continue my studies under Gainer's tutelage. I will always be indebted to her wisdom in sending me to Gainer.

After experiencing him firsthand in the classroom, I too saw why he was a legend. Even though both Musick and Gainer were passionate about folklore, their focuses were unique to their sense of place. Musick was an adopted West Virginian from the Sheridan Mountains of Missouri. Her fascination with folk narratives and songs extended into three areas: the Appalachian hills; the American frontier plains; and the Appalachian ethnic communities (especially the coal mines) inhabited by the southern Europeans who came into the Appalachians on the heels of the great industrial revolution of the early twentieth century. From her broad perspective, she gave me a love for the world tale.

Gainer's vision, however, was directly focused on the Allegheny Mountains of his birth. He was pure West Virginian, and his fierce mountain pride was contagious for all his students. His clear Irish tenor voice filled the room as he sang the traditional folk songs of his beloved state. Students jockeyed to secure places in his classes, which were considered for decades among the most popular in the English Department at WVU. I was honored to be among those students. Just to hear his singing ignited in me a love for my West Virginia, too!

Gainer belonged, in fact, to a series of renowned folklorists at West Virginia University who mined Appalachian culture, mostly in West Virginia, from about 1902 when John Harrington Cox came to Morgantown from Harvard until Gainer's retirement nearly three-quarters of a century later in 1972. The second member of the triumvirate, Louis Watson

Chappell, came to West Virginia University in 1922 and was a member of the English department for more than twenty-five years. His aluminum-disk collection of West Virginia fiddlers and balladeers, now known as the Louis Watson Chappell Archive at the West Virginia and Regional History Collection in the West Virginia Libraries, remains essential to the study of traditional music in Appalachia. Gainer, who had grown up with the folk music of his family, began his own serious study of folklore with Cox and Chappell when he was an undergraduate at West Virginia University in the 1920s. Later, Gainer returned to WVU after service in World War II with a doctorate from St. Louis University to teach in the English Department.

Ethnomusicology was certainly a focus of the research undertaken by Cox and Chappell. Cox produced *The Folksongs of the South* (Cambridge, MA: Harvard UP, 1925) as a result of his early West Virginia Folklore Society collecting, which remains important. Chappell published his still indispensable masterpiece of historical research, *John Henry: A Folklore Study* (Jena: Frommanche Verlag, 1933). In trying to preserve national characteristics perpetuated in the musical vernacular, these early folk scholars assembled a body of data and raw materials that would have been lost forever had they not collected it as well as their technologies would allow.

Moving into this atmosphere at West Virginia University, Gainer's love for folk music was enhanced by Cox and Chappell, from whom he was inspired to do his own folk song collecting. It is not surprising, then, that his primary legacy lies in the collecting, disseminating, and preserving of the Scots-Irish songs and ballads, especially the border ballads (first preserved in Francis James Child's *The English and Scottish Popular Ballads*) that were brought by the early settlers into the Appalachians. Next to Cecil Sharp who collected in the Carolina highlands, Gainer collected the most versions in Appalachia, which he published in his important text, *Folk Songs from the West Virginia Hills* (Morgantown: Seneca Books, 1975), and album, *Folk Songs of the Alleghenies* (Folk Heritage Recordings, 1963). Also in 1963, as part of the West Virginia Folklore Society's participation in the West Virginia Centennial, Gainer published a song book, *100 Centennial Songs of West Virginia* (WV: Governor's Centennial Council, 1963). These works demonstrate Gainer's devotion to two things: the music of his native West Virginia and his desire to reclaim the music from the ridicule it received beyond the state's borders in post-World War II America when our traditional music was labeled as "hillbilly."[1]

In 1975, Gainer also published the first edition of this book, *Witches, Ghosts and Signs* (Morgantown: Seneca Books), as a companion to *Folk Songs from the West Virginia Hills*. Its content represents the folkways that set the context for his beloved folk music. Reading this text is like being in Dr. Gainer's classes again. I can almost hear his voice in the layout of the phrases and sentences since the "Introduction" and opening notes to the sections come directly from his lectures and discussions. Published right after his retirement and only six years before his death, this book is Gainer's testimony to the values and beliefs of the Anglo-Celtic-Germanic settlers whose folklore has given Appalachia its identity in language patterns, customs, traditions, and beliefs. The great value of *Witches, Ghosts and Signs* is that it was not only the first, but remains the only body of scholarship thus far to catalog a rich variety of the customary lore and folk narratives of these early agrarian pioneers who began to settle in the heart of Appalachia before the American Revolution, and whose bloodlines can still be found in West Virginia.

Gainer possessed an innate understanding of the persona of the "proud mountaineer," for he had descended from the same cultural migration into these hills. His Celtic ancestors first came into central Appalachia in the early 1800s. Much of the customary lore in this text was supported by his own memories of growing up in Gilmer County among his vital grandparents with whom he and his mother made their home after the death of his own father when Gainer was still quite young. His Irish grandfather, F. C. Gainer, especially, sparked his love for singing the old ballads, spinning the strange tales, and abiding by the signs of nature. In his small community of Tanner with its surrounding environs, Gainer had personally participated in many of the traditional rural customs, such as bean stringing, quilting bees, and play parties, along with the other, more recognizable social occasions of Christmas and Halloween in the hills. These descriptions are extremely valuable to aid our understanding of the textual material passed

[1] There are MP3 files at http://www.libraries.wvu.edu/wvconline/patrickgainer.htm

on at such times. Of particular interest in our age of cell phones is Gainer's note on the Party Line (page 33), in which several families shared a single telephone line, sometimes singing to one another and very often snooping into lovers' quarrels and gossips' rumors.

Like a hymn to West Virginia's traditional folklore, the essence of the content resounds in the title: *Witches, Ghosts and Signs*. Witches and ghosts were common motifs in the storytelling traditions of the people who had brought many beliefs with them from their Anglo-Celtic-Germanic roots. These beliefs were reinforced by the patchy valley fog, shadowy topography, and isolated environment of the scattered homesteads and hill communities. In a typical mountain family, stories of the supernatural and the occult were common ways to "pass the time" while doing chores during the day or to entertain each other on long winter evenings as everyone gathered around the hearth. Gainer, himself a captivating storyteller, would often retell these ghostly and ghastly encounters from the perspective of the primary informant. In each telling he would insist that, "almost without exception, the people who told ghost tales to me believed in their actual existence." He was equally ambiguous about the reality of supernatural phenomena. When asked if he believed in their actual existence, he always replied with a twinkle in his eye, "It is more fun to believe!" In addition, he was philosophical about the signs of remedies, cures, omens, and tokens that influenced folk customs and behaviors, declaring with the same twinkle in his eye, "The only difference between superstition and belief is attitude!"

As valuable as this collection is to folklore scholarship, Gainer delighted in being able to use this book's introduction as a forum to defend Appalachian heritage against the misunderstandings of the "outside world" that dared to attack his "inside world" of West Virginia. He saw folklore as the best weapon to win what became his personal and intellectual war against the "hillbilly" stereotyping that branded Appalachia. Gainer aspired to present a clearer, more objective view of the Anglo-Celtic-Germanic people, the majority of whom were Scots-Irish descendents. In presenting their folkways, his mission was to dispel the attitudes that relegated these mountaineers into a subculture of ignorance and isolation. Gainer was especially incensed by "sociologically-related" writings, such as Harry Caudill's *Night*

Comes to the Cumberlands (Boston, 1962) that suggested "that proof of the ignorance of the mountaineers is their belief in witchcraft, preternatural phenomena, and superstitions." Gainer joined the chorus of a few other scholarly voices who were trying to define Appalachia to broader America, one of whom was Loyal Jones, director of the Appalachian Center at Berea College. The same year that *Witches, Ghosts and Signs* was published, Jones published an essay, "Appalachian Values," in *Voices From the Hills* (Ed. Robert J. Higgs and Ambrose Manning. New York: Unger, 1975), that supported Gainer's defense.

My last memories of Gainer are from 1975 to 1980 when we traveled to extension classes around the state presenting our chapters in B. B. Maurer's *Mountain Heritage* (Parsons, WV: McClain Printing, 1975). Gainer's chapter on music was an abridged version of his two books while mine was on folklore and literature, based on much that he and Musick had taught me. It was delightful to share time with Gainer as a colleague. He possessed the same Irish charm and wit that marked his teaching style years before. He also didn't miss any opportunity to denounce the negative stereotyping that clouded the traditional beauty of his mountain state. "Don't let anyone ever call you a Hillbilly," he warned his audiences. "A Hillbilly is a mountain goat. We are Mountaineers!"

Another benefit of the Maurer Lecture Series was that in 1977 we were videotaped in our presentations, so that a student's-eye view of Gainer remains available through our state library media services or from Jackson's Mill. This audio-visual source has been an important component to my teaching materials in my own folklore and folk literature classes, especially after Gainer's books ceased to be in print. My students have been able to hear him singing his beloved ballads and to see him telling his stories, always preaching the true value of the mountain culture.

Since Gainer was the ultimate "teacher scholar" whose contribution to the field of regional folklore studies provides such unique and important material, I am joyful to see *Witches, Ghosts and Signs* back in print. No longer will I have to collect copies from the library for my students to share. I am also happy that this second edition will provide an appendix that students can use in their research as models for their own collecting and that scholars and school programs, especially in the liberal arts, can use to identify narrative motifs and universal folkloric themes. My own students appreciated the opportunity to help develop the classification index that adds to the technical scholarship of the lore. I feel that the West Virginia University Press is publishing a powerful source through which future readers and students will continue to fully experience the charismatic essence of Dr. Patrick Gainer—scholar, teacher, performer, and crusader.

Dr. Gainer's family labored to get this project undertaken, and I am most appreciative that the West Virginia University Press was willing to take it on and to fund it with the scarce resources available today for publication. The interest that Dr. C. B. Wilson, associate provost of West Virginia University, took in the project helped drive it to completion, and the effort that Dr. Patrick Conner, Eberly College Centennial Professor in the Humanities and director of West Virginia University Press, gave to the project's realization was beyond the call of duty. Thank you, gentlemen! But most of all, I thank Dr. Patrick Ward Gainer for saving the fragments of our own history in our own words in his collection, and I urge everyone who is looking for a way to serve his or her community to emulate what he did. The study of the folk is always rewarded with a better knowledge of ourselves.

Dr. Judy Prozzillo Byers, Director
The Frank and Jane Gabor West Virginia Folklife Center
Abelina Suarez Senior Professor, English and Folklore Studies
Fairmont State University

Introduction
❖❖❖❖❖❖❖❖❖❖❖❖

The material presented in this volume has been collected from people in West Virginia over the last half-century.
Long before the tape recorder came into use, I was writing
down all kinds of traditional lore as I traveled over the hills and
through the hollows of the mountain state. This lore included
songs, instrumental music, dialectal speech, witch stories, ghost
stories, folk cures, nature lore, and superstitions. During most
of this time I was teaching large classes in folklore at West
Virginia University, both on the campus and in extension in
almost every region of the state. I also taught classes in folklore
at Glenville State College during the summers from 1950 to
1959. It was there that I originated the West Virginia State Folk
Festival in 1950. Students in my classes contributed much
material which they had collected in the field, and they gave
me many clues which led me to valuable sources of material.

Since the material in this book has come from the traditions
of the people who live among the hills and mountains of West
Virginia, people who are proud to be called mountaineers, I feel
that it is important to tell something about these people whose
ancestors chose as the motto of their state, "Mountaineers Are
Always Free." Perhaps we can help to correct the misconception regarding the character of the mountain people, which one
gains from much that is written in fiction, magazine articles,

books by sociologically-oriented writers, and on radio and television, where "Appalachia" is characterized as a land of "hillbillies," where there is poverty, depression, loneliness, and ignorance.

The West Virginia "hillbilly" is pictured as a kind of degenerate character whose chief occupation is making moonshine. He wears no shoes, wears dirty, ragged clothes, a ragged hat with a pointed crown, and is usually depicted asleep near his moonshine still or sitting on the porch of his little shack while his woman does the work. To true West Virginia mountaineers, the term "hillbilly" is highly derogatory and insulting.

It is unfortunate that Harry M. Caudill, in his description of the people of the Cumberland Plateau region of Kentucky, "a serrated upland in the eastern and southeastern region of the state," generalizes when he summarizes his characterization of the mountaineers in Chapter 2 of his book:

> The illiterate son of illiterate ancestors, cast loose in an immense wilderness without basic mechanical or agricultural skills, without the refining, comforting and disciplining influence of an organized religious order, in a vast land wholly unrestrained by social organization or effective laws, compelled to acquire skills quickly in order to survive, and with a Stone Age savage as his principal teacher.
>
> From these forces emerged the mountaineer as he is to an astonishing degree even to this day.[1]

Mr. Caudill suggests that proof of the ignorance of the mountaineers is their belief in witchcraft, preternatural phenomena, and superstitions:

> In the loneliness and mid the brooding silences of the great forest, this hodgepodge of superstition was called upon to give the explanations of the mysteries and the consolations for the miseries for which mankind has, in all ages, turned to his priests.

[1]Harry M. Caudill, Night Comes to the Cumberlands (Boston, 1962), p. 31.

Much of the life on the frontier has superstitious over-
tones, and countless commonplace occurrences were
carefully studied for meaning or portent. Witchcraft enjoyed widespread credence and misfortune was likely to
be attributed to a spell. This in turn called for much con-
jecture on the question of the witch's identity.[2]

Mr. Caudill is, of course, writing about the people of a certain
region of the southern mountains, the Cumberland Plateau region of Kentucky. However, when he refers to the "mountaineers" without restricting the term to the people of a certain
region of the mountains, most readers will unfortunately conclude that his characterization applies to all mountaineers of
the Southern Appalachian Mountains.

The belief in witchcraft, superstitions, and supernatural
phenomena is universal and ancient. Many people who have
told me stories of witches often cite the account of the Witch
of Endor in the Old Testament, in First Kings, chapter 28, verse
7 and following: "And Saul said to his servants, 'Seek me a
woman that hath a divining spirit, and I will go to her.' And his
servants said to him, 'There is a woman that lives at Endor that
hath a divining spirit.' And Saul disguised himself and went to
the woman at Endor. And she brought forth the spirit of Samuel."

I do not believe there is any greater belief in witchcraft
among the mountain people than there is in any other part of
the world. It was not in the mountains of Southern Appalachia
that almost two dozen women were put to death because they
were convicted of the crime of witchcraft; it was in New England, the great center of intellectual power in Colonial America. It is in the great urban centers of America that people spend
millions of dollars each year going to the numerous quacks who
claim to have the power to bring the spirits of the dead back to
earth. It is in our large American cities that numerous "covens"
of witches have organized in this seventh decade of the twen-

[2] *Ibid.*, p. 26.

tieth century. In large American cities, such as New York,
Chicago, Pittsburgh, and St. Louis, I have seen living conditions
far more deplorable than I have seen in the hills of West Virginia. It is no more reasonable to characterize the mountaineers
as ignorant, lazy, and impoverished people because of some
scattered shacks occupied by shiftless, lazy people, than it
would be to characterize the people of these large cities as
impoverished and lazy because of the existence of deplorable
ghettos.

If the reader wishes to know more about the people of the
Mountain State, he should read *West Virginia the Mountain
State,* written by two West Virginia University professors,
Charles H. Ambler and Festus P. Summers, published by Pren-
tice-Hall, 1965. I recommend especially chapters I, V, IX, XIII,
and XX.

The people who first came into the region that was later
named West Virginia were mostly of German, English, Irish,
and Scotch ancestry. Many of our ancestors came to America in
the early part of the eighteenth century, and many of them
fought in the Revolutionary War. Many German people came
into the Shenandoah Valley from Pennsylvania and later moved
west over the Allegheny Mountains. Many of the English came
into Virginia and thence west over the mountains to the west-
ern foothills. Many of the Irish and Scotch came into Maryland,
thence south and west into and over the mountains to the west.
This was true of my own paternal ancestors, who came to America in 1725 and were land owners in southern Maryland until
the early part of the nineteenth century, when they moved
south over the old Seneca Trail into what was then Randolph
County, Virginia, now West Virginia.

These people were farmers; they moved west into the Allegheny Mountains and the valleys of the foothills stretching
west to the Ohio Valley, because there was much land to be
bought at low prices, and they sought freedom from the oppres-
sion of rich land owners, which they had experienced in the
old-world environment. They came to the hill country, where

they found rich bottom lands for grain and meadows, and fertile hillsides to be turned into bluegrass pasture.

They could bring with them only the things most necessary for living, but they knew how to build houses and furnish them with home-made furniture. They knew how to grow flax to be turned into linen clothing; and they could spin and weave the wool from the sheep which they raised. They brought few books besides the Bible, but in their minds they carried a great store of traditional knowledge, and in their hearts a love for the best that had been said in story and song by their ancestors for countless generations. Even the language they used was largely that which had been preserved in oral tradition. Some of the words which they used had not changed since the time of Chaucer.

These pioneers were religious people. Even before they had time to build churches, they would clear out a patch of woods for a meeting place, leaving stumps of trees for seats. Gradually villages formed, and these became centers where people came to buy certain items which could not be produced on the land, such as coffee and salt. Typical of these centers was Tanner, Gilmer County, near which I grew up. At the beginning of this century the little village had a hotel, two general stores, a hardware store, a barber shop, two blacksmith shops, a medical doctor who conducted his practice in an office, two churches, a large flour mill, a school, and a good brass band complete with a bandwagon, on which the musicians traveled to other communities and to the county fair each year in August. Singing teachers came once or twice a year and taught the people to read music so as to be able to sing the old songs in four-part harmony. There was a monthly gathering at the schoolhouse, called a "literary," which brought people in from miles around to take part in such activities as debates, dramas, readings, and orations. In harvest time people gathered at each other's homes to help with the work of threshing, stringing beans, peeling apples, shucking corn, and making molasses. Besides being work sessions, these were great social gatherings also.

These people did not have much in the way of cash money, nor did they need much. Most of the buying of necessities at the store was done by bartering eggs, chickens, butter, rabbits, ginseng, hides, and other products, for store goods.

On long winter evenings there was time to gather before the fireplace to sing songs and tell stories, and to exchange ideas. If a stranger came by, he was welcome to stay the night and sit at the board with the family for a good supper and breakfast. Stories were told of ghosts and witches, of pioneer days and unusual incidents. The stories of witches and ghosts were not told so much to make others believe in these things, but because these stories were an entertaining feature of the oral literature of the folk. Our society today needs books, recordings, radio, and television for our entertainment and knowledge, for we retain very little in our minds to pass on to others. There is very little remaining in our modern society in the way of oral tradition. Our pioneer ancestors, however, did not need books as much as our modern society needs them, for they preserved in their minds a treasury of knowledge, of fiction, of poetry as song, ready to be passed on to their children and grandchildren.

Today there are many people who think that the people who live in the hills are suspicious of "outsiders" and receive them with hostility. In all my travels over the hills and through the hollows for half a century, recording folklore and encouraging people to be proud of their heritage, never have I encountered any sign of hostility, but always a genuine show of friendliness.

Speech of the Mountaineers
✤✤✤✤✤✤✤✤✤✤✤✤✤✤✤✤✤✤✤✤✤✤✤✤✤✤✤✤

When we study the speech of the people of the hills and mountains, we must keep in mind that not all people of this region speak alike. We are studying *traditional* speech which has survived in our traditions for centuries. There have been more changes in this speech in the last seventy years than there were in two centuries before that. The loss of traditional dialect and the standardization of our speech are the result of several causes:

The development of education has been a leading factor. Fifty years ago comparitively few young people attended high school, for there were very few high schools in existence.

At the beginning of this century, people living in rural areas had very few daily papers to read, and almost no magazines.

Radio, which has done much to standardize speech, did not become common until the third decade of this century.

Finally, television has probably been the greatest influence on speech in recent years.

People are far less provincial today than they were at the beginning of the century. With good roads running through all sections of the mountains, people travel much more. They go to the cities to do most of their buying. This fact, along with the consolidation of schools, explains the break-up of community life, for in former days the village was the center of much social life. The country school and the singing school preserved and generated much social and intellectual activity. Today the television set holds the attention of most people, with the result that everyone is listening to the same standardized speech.

I have heard "outsiders" say that in the Appalachian Mountains the people speak a pure Elizabethan language. This is far from the truth. In talking with elderly people, one might hear some traditional speech containing a few words that could be recognized as Chaucerian, such as "fernint," "liever," and "found." However, for the most part the language would be completely modern. It is true that it would not sound the same as the speech one might hear in New York, New England, Pittsburgh, or Chicago, for the accents would vary. Even within the boundaries of the state of West Virginia, one may hear several distinctly different accents.

The study of dialectal speech is difficult today because of the problems the collector encounters in the field. The student of speech must become one with the people if he is to hear them speaking in a natural manner. When the collector lets it be known that he is collecting examples of speech, and sets up his tape recorder for the purpose, he immediately creates an artificial situation, which tends to inhibit people from using the speech they would normally use in the family circle or even in the country general store.

Those collectors who wish to be accepted by the people of the region should never attempt to imitate the speech of the people. One can never accomplish this unless he has spent many years with the people. If a speaker uses a dialectal pronunciation of a word, one must never repeat the word with a different pronunciation. For example, if the speaker says "crick," one should not pronounce the word "creek." If a speaker says, "Have you heerd the song about the groundhog?"—one should never say, "No, I have not *heard* it." This embarrasses the speaker by causing him to feel that he is not pronouncing the word correctly. It is better to avoid using the word.

It is impossible to do much research in traditional speech by mail. It is almost useless to send out questionaires, asking people to indicate what name they might give to a certain object, listing several choices. In most instances, the person who answers the questionaire will mark the example which he knows to be correct, and not the one he might have heard his grandparents use.

To study the speech of the people, one must go into the field and get to *know* the *people*. Above all, one must not take the attitude that he is studying the illiterate speech of an ignorant people; it is a *traditional* speech that has been preserved in oral tradition for centuries, just as songs, stories, and a vast treasury of knowledge have all been preserved in the minds and hearts of the people.

DIALECT AND ACCENT

Dialect is the language of the people of a particular region, as distinguished from the standard language. Dialect is speech that has lived in oral tradition, as distinguished from standard language, which is preserved in written form.

The word *accent* refers to the characteristic pronunciation of words. If one's speech is made up entirely of standard words, his speech is not dialect. However, if he pronounces these words in a manner characteristic of one particular region, he is said to have an accent. For example, the word *been* may be pronounced as "bin," "be-ĕn," "bean," or "bĕn," depending on the environmental influence on the language of the speaker.

Dialect and accent are not the result of race but of environment. The speech of a black person is not different from that of a white person if both have had the same environment since infancy. People who learn to speak English after having spoken a foreign language exclusively for many years, may retain certain characteristic sounds of their mother tongue. Thus in America we have such distinguishing accents, such as German-

English, Italian-English, French-English, and many others. These distinguishing accents are purely environmental, however. Family influence is very strong in determining speech habits, which explains why there are varying accents in one community, if different families of the community have not lived there for the same length of time.

Probably the most distinguishing characteristic of the speech of the people of the Southern Appalachians is the slurring of the vowel so that it becomes a diphthong. It is a traditional accent which comes from the highland country of Scotland and Northern England. The poet Tennyson uses this Northern English speech in his poem, "Northern Farmer, Old Style." There is very little difference between the speech of Tennyson's northern farmer, who speaks in a monologue, and that of elderly men whom we have often heard in the hills of West Virginia.

All vowels are likely to be pronounced as diphthongs. It is difficult to reproduce the exact sound in writing, but we are indicating the vowel sound thus:

> *bad* is bă-ŭd
> *been* is bĕ-ŭn
> *and* is ă-ŭnd
> *end* is ĕ-ŭnd
> *did* is dĭ-ŭd
> *door* is dō-ŭr
> *bud* is bŭ-ŭd

Vowel sounds may vary, and these variations may be heard in the speech of one person, even in the same sentence. For example, "there" and "thär," and "here" and "hyŭr" may occur in the speech of one person.

Words ending in *-ow* are usually pronounced as if ending in *-er. Hollow* becomes *holler, meadow* becomes *medder,* and *fellow* becomes *feller.*

The letter *a* on the end of a word becomes a *y. Soda* is *sody, Orma* is *Ormy, Sarah* is *Sarry,* and *Virginia* is *Virginny.*

The sound of the consonant *r* is often heard within a word but never at the end of a word to replace the sound of *a*. Thus *bush* may be pronounced *boorsh*, *push* is *poorsh*, *daughter* is *dorter*, and *ought* is *ort*.

The final *d* of a word is often pronounced as *t*. *Hold* is *holt*, *salad* is *salat*, *ballad* is *ballat*, and *tend* is *tent*.

The present participle of almost all verbs is prefixed by the sound of *a* as in sálūte. "He's *a-goin'* home," "The flowers are all *a-dyin'*." Sometimes the past participle is also prefixed by this same sound, as in "I've *a-turned* eighty-five already," or "He's *a-gone* and left home."

The vowel *a* is usually given a short sound, as in *hălf*, *călf*, and *dănce*. However, the *a* sound may be broad as in *äunt* (usually so pronounced in Logan County) and *cläpboard*.

Short *ĕ* is sometimes pronounced as short *i*, as in *git*, *yisterday*, and *yit*. Short *ĕ* is also sometimes pronounced as long *ā*, when *ĕgg* becomes *āig* and *lĕg* becomes *lāig*.

Short *ĭ* frequently becomes long *ē*, as in *feesh*, *deesh*, and *weesh*. This pronunciation is especially true of central and southern West Virginia speech.

Short *ĭ* is also often pronounced as short *ĕ*, when *sĭnce* becomes *sĕnce*: "It's been a long time sence I've seen you." *Sĭng* becomes *sĕng*: "I like to sĕng the old songs."

Long *ī* is often pronounced as broad *ä*: "Äh don't care." *Nīne* becomes *nähn*, *tīre* is *tähr*, *fīre* is *fähr*, and *īron* is *ährn* or *airn*.

Long *ō* often sounds like *āo*, as in *gāo* for *gō*.

Short *ŭ* has various pronunciations. Sometimes it becomes short *ĭ*, as it *jist* for *jŭst*. It may become short *ĕ* as in *shĕt* for *shŭt* or *brĕsh* for *brŭsh*. It becomes *ōō* in *bōōsh* for *bŭsh*, *cōōshion* for *cŭshion*, and *pōōsh* for pŭsh.

The diphthong *oi* is likely to be pronounced as long *ī*. *Spoil* is *spīle*, *point* is *pīnt*, *boil* is *bīle*, and *oil* is *īle*.

The diphthong *ou* is sometimes pronounced as *hāouse* and *abāout*. This is true in southern West Virginia and Virginia.

Words ending in *ing* usually omit the final *g*. "Are you a-goin' to singin' tonight?"

WORDS AND EXPRESSIONS

aback (adv.), back. "The well is aback of the house."

abed (adv.), in bed. "Pa's been sick abed for a week."

abide (v.), tolerate. "I can't abide lazy people."

admire (v.), to wonder at. "I admired how tall that building was."

afeard (adj.), afraid. "My wife's afeard of the dark."

affecting (adj.), given to false show. "I like a girl that acts natural. That one is too affecting."

afore (adv.), before. "I'll get there afore the train comes in."

ageé (adj.), awry. "That span of rail fence is all ageé."

agin (adv.), against or before. "Agin I get the work done, it'll be too late to go."

ahīnt (adv.), behind. "Look what's ahint you."

ailin' (v.) not feeling well. "Granny's ailin' agin."

aim (v.), to plan. "I aim to build a barn this summer."

allow or *'low* (v.), to think. "I 'low it'll rain today."

allus (adv.), always. "I allus did like cornbread."

alter (v.), to castrate an animal. "The sign is not right to alter the hogs."

anear (adv.), near. "The well is anear the house."

ary (adj.), any. "Will there be ary seat for us?"

amód (v.), change, or revise. "If I don't like the words of the song, I just amód it."

ax (v.), ask. "I aim to ax her to marry me."

back a letter (verb phrase), to write the address on the envelope of a letter. "I want you to back this letter for me."

back-log (n.), the large log placed in the rear of the fireplace. "The back-log ort to burn all night."

backset (n.), relapse. "We thought Mary was better, but she tuk a backset."

bad-off (adj.), ill. "They say Will's bad-off with the fever."

beaslings (n.), the first milk of a cow after the birth of a calf. "If you milk the beaslings on the ground, the cow will go dry."

beat time (v.), to win a girl's favor from another fellow. "John was goin' with Mary, but Bill beat his time."

bees are goin' to swarm (n. clause), a baby is expected. "They're expectin' the bees to swarm over at the Daly's."

biggity (adj.), snobbish. "Since Charlie's been to the city, he's got powerful biggity."

blinky (adj.), sour. "This milk has got blinky."

bodacious (adj.), intensive adjective. "He's a bodacious liar."

bodaciously (adv.), utterly. "The sheep got in the wheat and et it bodaciously up."

boughten (adj.), purchased at a store. "She's wearin' a boughten dress."

bōged (adj.), tired, exhausted. "I worked till I was boged."

bollix (v.), to mess, to ruin. "We had a good deal a-goin', but he bollixed it up."

brash (adj.), windy and cold, referring to weather. "That weather is right brash out there today."

bring (v.), produce. "That land ort to bring a good crop."

broke (v.), changed for worse in physical condition. "Will has broke a lot since I last saw him."

brung (v), brought. "The cattle brung a good price."

buck-agers (n.), state of nervousness. "His speech was all right, but he had the buck-agers." (Probably from *ague*, a fever which causes chills and shaking.

bullnozer (n.), bulldozer. "They can make a sight of road with that bullnozer."

call (n.), reason, occasion. "You have no call to insult him." "There's no call to talk like that."

care (v.), to object. "Will you eat with us?" If the reply is, "I don't care," it means, "Yes, I'll be glad to."

carry (v.), to escort. "May I carry you home?"

chance (n.), large number or amount. "He has a right smart chance of cattle in the pasture."

chaw (n.) chew. "He took a chaw of tobaccer."

chawed (v.), past tense of chew. "Sam allus chawed his own-grown tobaccer."

chillern or *chillun* (n.), children. "The chillern are all gone."

chippie (n.), a prostitute. "She's got her face painted up like a chippie."

church (v.), to be churched is to be expelled from membership in the church. "Jim Boggs was brought before the elders last week, and they churched him."

churching (n.), the churching (purification) of a mother after the birth of a child. Observed by some Catholics in America, but not by Protestants. The word is rare in America.

clean (adv.), entirely, completely. "The bullet went clean through his leg." "The horses pulled the wagon clean to the top of the hill."

clift (n.) cliff. "Jimmy clumb up the rock clift and fell off."

clunch (n.), perfume. "Who's a-wearin' all that clunch?"

clumb (v.), past tense of climb. "He clumb a tree."

common (adj.), affable, friendly, genteel. "That professor is mighty common." Common is a complimentary term.

coverlid (n.), woven bedspread. "My grandma wove the coverlid for my bed."

crick (n.), creek. "The crick's up too much to ford it."

cut a wide swath (v. phrase), to try to do more than one is able to do. "He's a-tryin' to cut a wide swath."

cut out (v.), to take another fellow's girl. "Lucy was Bob's girl till Ezra cut him out."

dássent (v.), dare not. "The crick is so high I dassent ford it."

dauncy (adj.), not in good health. "Sarry's been a leetle dauncy here lately."

deal (n.), large amount. "He has a deal of money."

deef (adj.), deaf. "He's deef in one ear."

dike up (v.), to dress up. "There's no need to dike up just to go to the store." (adj.) "He was all diked up in his best clothes."

do (v.), to cheat or outwit. "If you don't watch him, he'll do you."

doctor-medicine (n.), medicine prescribed by a doctor, as contrasted with herb medicine or folk cure. "He tried doctor-medicine for his rheumatism, but it did him no good."

doins (n.), a party or a gathering of people. "There's to be a big doins at the church next Sunday."

dornick (n.), stone. "He hit him with a dornick."

drap (n.), for drop, or small amount. "I'd like a drap of whiskey."

dreckly (adv.), directly, in a short time. "I'll be there dreckly."

drene (v.), to drain. "You ought to drene the water off the beans."

dud (v.), to remove the clothes. "You got your clothes all wet; you'd better dud yourself before the fire."

due-bill (n.), a statement indicating the amount of money due from the store when bartering eggs, butter, etc. "The storekeeper gave me a due-bill for my eggs."

fair-to-middlin' (adj.), moderately well in health. "Grandma's been fair-to-middlin' this week."

fair up (v.), for the weather to become fair. "I 'low it will fair up by noon."

falbala (n.) furbelow. A beautiful flowering bush was called a falbala. "I want you to see my falbala behind the house."

family-way (n.), pregnant. "My wife is in the family-way."

farce (v.), to stuff. "My daughter-in-law knows little about cooking; she can't even farce a chicken." (Chaucer's friar had his hood *farced* full of knives and pins.)

fault (v.), to blame. "He broke the axe handle, but I didn't fault him for it."

favor (v.), to resemble. "The boy favors his father."

faze or *feeze* (v.), to daunt or bother. "The rock hit him on the head, but it didn't faze him."

fernint (adv.), opposite. "The barn is acrost the road fernint the house."

fice (n.), (sometimes *penny-fice*) feist, a small dog. To call one a penny-fice means that he is one who makes much noise that amounts to little. "The politician is nothing but a penny-fice."

filth (n.), brush and weeds growing in pasture land. "I cut filth all day yesterday." The word *filth* is used in this way only in West Virginia.

fire-board (n.), mantel. "The lamp is on the fire-board."

fix (v.), to be pregnant. "Miz Barb's in a fix agin."

fit (v.) past tense of *fight*. "They fit a hard battle."

fodder-beans (n.), dried string beans, also called *leather-brit-ches*. "We had a mess of fodder-beans cooked with fat pork."

for (prefix), very or extremely. "He left his for-true-love be-hind."

forestick (n.), small log placed in the front part of the fireplace. "You forgot to put the forestick on before you started the fire."

foughten (adj.), past participle of *fight*. "It was a hard foughten scrap."

found (n.), board and room. "I give my work hands a dollar a day and found."

founder (v.), to become ill from over-eating. "If you eat all that cake, you'll founder yourself."

freshen (v.), to bear a calf. "The cow will freshen in May."

funny (adj.), strange. "We thought it was funny to see so many stars fall."

fur piece (n.), long distance. "It's a fur piece to the next town."

furriner (n.), foreigner. A person from another region is a fur-riner. One from a foreign country is a "durn furriner." "He pears to me like a furriner."

gab (v.), gossip. "That woman gabs too much."

galluses (n.), suspenders. "I wear galluses to hold my breeches up."

ganted (adj.), ill used. (said of a horse) "That horse has been worked so hard he looks ganted."

garden-house (n.), privy, outhouse. "In winter time it gets too cold to go to the garden-house."

get religion (v.), to be converted to Christianity. "Ike got reli-gion at the big meetin' last night."

glister (v.), glitter. "I saw a light glister a mile away."

glom (v.), to make a mess of something. "The little girl tried to make a dress, but she glommed it all up."

grabble (v.), to take the young potatoes from the ground when they are large enough to cook, leaving the smaller ones in the ground to mature. "Go out in the garden and grabble a mess of potatoes."

grass-widow (n.), a woman who is separated from her husband but not divorced. "They tell me that young woman who has just come to town is a grass-widow."

guinea (n.), someone foreign to the community. It is a derogatory term, usually applied to one of mixed racial origin. "I don't want that young fellow seein' my daughter, for he's a guinea."

gritchel (n.), a small traveling bag. "She carried her things in a gritchel."

hackin' (n.), the underbrush. "He's workin' in the hackin'."

hard-favored (adj.), not handsome. "He's a hard-favored man."

hant (n.), ghost or spirit. "I relly believe it was a hant."

hardness (n.), ill feeling. "There's hardness between the two families."

harry (v.), to harrow. "I aim to harry the field today."

hate (n.), "I don't give a hate" means "I don't care." "I don't give a hate what you do."

heap (n.), large quantity. "He has a heap of money."

hear to (v.), agree to. "He would never hear to that kind of settlement."

helligan (n.), bad storm. "We'd better get to the house, for there's a helligan a-comin'."

hellion (n.), a young boy who makes trouble. "That youngun is a regular hellion."

hell-roarin'-trots (n.), diarrhea. "Too much green corn will give you the hell-roarin'-trots."

het up (adj.), aroused, angry. "He is all het up about it."

hippen (n.), diaper. "That baby needs a new hippen."

hired-girl (n.), a girl who is hired to work regularly in the home, usually living with the family. "We have a good hired-girl."

hired-man (n.), a man who is hired to work regularly on the farm, usually living in a separate house on the farm. "The hired-man is a mighty good worker."

hit (pronoun), it. "Hit looks like rain."

holler (n.), hollow. "Pa went up the holler to try to get a deer." *Holler* also means a combination of tones set to words or nonsense syllables, which a young man uses to identify himself, especially when he is approaching the home of his girl after dark. "There comes Jim, I know him by his holler."

holp (v.), help. "I'll come over and holp you tomorrow."

hooly (adv.), slowly, deliberately. "Hooly she got up." Used in song but rarely in speech.

howdy (v.), to greet one. "We've howdied, but we ain't shuck." This means, "We've spoken, but we haven't shaken hands."

hursh (v.), hush, keep quiet. "Hursh your mouth."

hunker (v.), to squat or to sit on haunches. "I hunkered down behind a bush and waited for him."

hussif (n.), a rectangular-shaped piece of cloth, often hand-woven, with pockets sewed on it in which to keep needles, thread, and thimbles. "Aunt Sarry kept her hussif hangin' at the left of the fireplace."

hyped-up (adj.), when a jacket does not fit well between the shoulders, it is hyped-up. "Your coat is all hyped-up in the back."

hyur (adv.), here. "Come out hyur on the porch."

iffen (conj.), if. "Iffen it rains, I won't go."

infare (n.), the celebration when the newly married couple first move into their home. "They had a big infare when Marg and Fran got married." From Old English: *in* plus *faren,* to go.

ingarns (n.), onions. "I allus plant my ingarns in March."

jist (adv.), simply, quite. "The shoes fit jist right."

juberous (adj.), doubtful. Probably a corruption for *dubious.* "I'm a little juberous about riding that horse."

jump (v.), to accuse. "He jumped me about spending too much."

keep (n.), caution, care. "Take keep you don't get hurt."

keerpet (n.), carpet. "Grandma wove a keerpet for the little room."

kittle (n.), kettle. "Put a kittle of water on to bile."

lappin' (n.), whipping. "The teacher gave Harry a lappin'."

lickin' (n.), whipping. "The boys had a fight, and Joe got a lickin'."

larn (v.), to learn or to teach. "You can't larn an old dog new tricks."

larpin' (adv.), very, exceedingly. "This pie is larpin' good."

law (v.), to sue in court. "He lawed me because he said my fence was on his land."

laylock (n.), lilac. "We've a laylock growing in the yard."

lay off (v.) to procrastinate. "I've laid off goin' to town for a week."

leastun (n.), the youngest one. "He's the leastun of the family."

leedle (adv.), little. "He's a leedle taller nor me."

let on (v.), to divulge. "I didn't let on that I am a Democrat."

liever (adv.), rather. "I'd liever be a Democrat than a Republican."

light (v.), to dismount from a horse. "Light and come in."

light-bread (n.), bread made of wheat flour with yeast. "I like a mess of light-bread now and then."

likely (adj.), capable. "The big feller is the likely one to do the job."

line out (v.), to teach a song by rote, line by line. "The preacher fetched a new song and lined it out for us at the meetin'."

literary (n.), a meeting at the school at night, when the pupils and the country folk joined in activities, such as debating, drama, reading, singing, etc. "Every first Wednesday night of the month we had a literary at our school."

lopper-jawed (adj.), lopsided. "Your hat's on lopper-jawed."

mackly (adj.), spotted or soiled. "Jenny got her dress all mackly."

make (v.), to become. "He went to the normal school to make a teacher."

mess (n.), a sufficient quantity for a meal. "We had our first mess of beans today."

mincy (adj.), particular in eating. "The little girl won't eat much; she's too mincy."

mind (v.), remember. "Do you mind when we went to school together?"

mitten (n.), when a young lady refused the young man who asked to see her home, it was said that she gave him the mitten. "Jim asked Mary to see her home last night, but she gave him the mitten."

Miz (title), for *Mrs.* "Miz Greene had several children."

mommick (v.), to ruin something by botching it up. "Susan cut out a dress, but she mommicked it up."

mourner (n.), at a revival meeting, one who is seeking religion but has not yet been converted. "Uncle Fud sat on the mourner's bench at the meetin' last night."

nary (adv.), not any. "He had nary a cent."

nearder (adv.), nearer. "You're nearder to the door than I am."

nigh (adv.) near. "It is nigh on to noon." (adj.), "There's a nigh cut over the hill."

nor (conj.), than. "He's a better fiddler nor me."

nother (adv.), neither. "Iffen you don't go, nother will I."

nubbin (n.), a small ear of corn. "My corn turned out to be mostly nubbins this year."

nuss (v.), to hold a child on one's lap. "Come here, let me nuss you, and I'll sing you a song."

old (adj.), a term of endearment. "The old woman is a mighty good cook." "Old Charlie is a fine work horse."

outsider (n.), one who is foreign to the region. "These outsiders come in here and tell us how to live."

pack (v.), to carry. "Let me pack your books for you."

passel (n.), parcel, portion. "He got a passel of land from his father." "Mother baked a passel of pies."

painter (n.), panther. "He was attacked by a painter."

patteridge (n.), partridge. "He shot a patteridge with his new gun."

pears (v.), appears. "It pears like rain."

peart (adj.), lively, in good health. "I've been right peart all week." *Peart* may also mean to insult, "Don't you peart me."

piece (n.), distance. "It's only a little piece from here."

pint (n.), point. "He lives on the pint yonder."

pintedly (adv.), firmly. "He pintedly believes it."

pitched off (v.), left hurriedly. "When it began to rain, he pitched off for home."

play-party (n.), a social gathering where singing games are played. "There's to be a play-party at Rufner's come Saturday night."

poke (n.), sack or bag. "I bought a poke of flour at the store." "I bought a poke of candy for the younguns."

poke (v.), to go slow. "When you go to the store, don't poke."

porely (adj.), in poor health. "Ma is porely agin today."

powerful (adv.), very. "There was a powerful big storm."

prin nearly (adv.), almost. "He choked her prin nearly to death."

press (n.), a closet for keeping clothes, linens, etc. "His suit looks like it has just come out of the press."

prize (v.), pry. "They were prizin' under the logs."

proud (adj.), pleased. "I am proud to meet you."

purt nigh (adv.) fairly near. "It's purt nigh to midnight."

purties (n.), play things, keepsakes. "The girl has lots of purties in her room."

put away (v.), to bury the dead. "They tuk Pa through that door when they put him away."

quile (n.), coil. "Fetch that quile of rope with you."

quorl (n.), cluster. "I found a quorl of yellowroot near that big rock."

raisin' (n.), bringing-up, training. "That boy acts like he's had no raisin'."

rare (v.), to scold. "Pa rared me when I broke the shovel."

reckon (v.), to think, suppose. "I reckon we'll have snow today."

red up (v.), to tidy up. "I ought to red up the house today."

red-man (v.), to punish without legal process, by vigilante organization. "They red-manned Si Tenner because he was allus beatin' his wife."

rench (v.), rinse. "I have to rench out the clothes."

retch (v.), reached. "I retched out and caught him before he could fall."

rid (v.), past tense of *ride*. "We rid ten miles yisterday."

right (adv.) fairly. "I'm right peart today." "The wind was right brash yesterday."

sang (n.), ginseng. To go "sangin'" is to hunt for ginseng in the woods. "I aim to go sangin' today."

sassengers (n.), sausages. "I like to eat saurkraut and sassengers."

scours (n.), diarrhea. "The cows have the scours."

scutchin' (n.), beating. "He got a scutchin' in town."

see (v.), to escort, literally to protect. "May I see you home?" "May God see you and save you."

seed (v.), past tense of *see*. "I seed him in town today."

shoe-mouth-deep (adj.), "The snow is shoe-mouth-deep." This means that the snow is as deep as the mouth of a man's shoe.

servagerous (adj.), very active. "That youngun is too servagerous to suit me. I can't keep up with him."

settin-up (n.), a wake for the dead. "When Uncle Isaac died, they had a big settin'-up for him."

shammick (v.), to walk slowly. "Bill didn't want to leave, but he finally shammicked off home."

shet (v.), shut. "Get up and shet the door."

shuck-pullin' (n.), corn-husking party. "There's goin' to be a shuck-pullin' at Hart's barn tonight."

shindig (n.), square-dance. "They cleaned out the old barn and had a big shindig."

sight (n.), large number or amount. "We had a sight of butter from that one churning."

slew (n.), large number. "There was a whole slew of people at the sale."

snaps (n.), string beans. "We picked a mess of snaps for dinner."

snede (n.), the handle of a scythe. "I like a scythe with a light snede."

sniptious (adj.), handsome, becoming. "That suit looks sniptious."

snits (n.), apples quartered for drying or making apple butter. "We've already cut enough snits to make five gallons of butter."

sop (v.), to dip bread in gravy or coffee. "I like to sop my bread in my coffee."

sop (n.), gravy or sauce. "This ham gravy makes a good sop."

sorry (adj.), inferior. "That is a sorry horse."

spang (adv.) exactly. "He fell spang in the middle of the mudhole."

spell (n.), a period of time. "We may have a dry spell."

spell (n.), illness. "Granny had a bad spell last week."

spit-and-image (n.), exactness, likeness. "The baby is the spit-and-image of his pappy."

stint (v.), to stop. "Don't stint till you've gone all the way home."

stout (adj.), overweight. "You'll get too stout if you don't work."

stoved (adj.), incapacitated. "That horse got stoved from being rid down hill too fast."

swear a baby (v. phrase), To name the father of an illegitimate baby. "She never swore her baby to anyone."

swingletree (n.), singletree. "The off-horse jerked so hard he broke the swingletree."

tally (v.), to charge something at the store. "Get some coffee at the store, and tell them to tally it."

tent (v.), to attend to. "I have to go on the hill and tent the cattle."

tenter (v.), to tie up. "Be sure you tenter your horse so he won't run away."

thar (adv.), there. "Put the horse over thar in the barn."

tollable (adj.), fairly well, referring to state of health. "I'm right tollable today, thank you."

tother (adj.), the other. "I saw him just tother day."

tō-tore (adj.), (pronounced *toe,* plus *tore*) torn to pieces. *To* is an intensive prefix, as in Middle English. "He got in the brier patch and got his breeches to-tore up."

traipse (v.), to go from place to place. "I had to traipse all over the hills to find the cows."

tuk (v.), took. "He tuk for home in a hurry."

tuk him with some papers (v. phrase), served legal papers. "The sheriff tuk him with some papers so he had to go to court."

turn (n.), a piece of work. "I did a turn in the hay today."

tursh (n.), tusk or tooth. "The dog put his tursh right through the man's hand."

uppards (adv.), almost. "We got uppards of twenty bushels of corn from that little patch."

varmint (n.), an unwanted creature, sometimes a human being. "Some varmint stole three of my chickens."

yon (adj.), yonder. "He lives in yon house."

yonderin' (adj.), something that wanders, such as a stream. "I last saw your horse along that yonderin' stream."

zounds (interjection), a mild oath, an abbreviation of "God's wounds."

Traditional
Activities and Customs
❖❖❖❖❖❖❖❖❖❖❖❖❖❖❖❖❖❖❖❖❖❖❖❖

Many people have been led to believe that the mountaineers lived a very lonely life, with little opportunity for social life. Although this was obviously true in the early colonial days when the region was being settled, it has not been the case for more than a century. The mountaineer, living in his cabin up a hollow or on a lonely ridge, surrounded by vast forests at least a mile from his nearest neighbor, is a character well-known in fiction and in the comic strip, but a rarity in real life.

In the following section, I describe some of the numerous community activities which were part of the traditions of the people in rural West Virginia until the third decade of this century. When we use the word *community* we mean an area that includes all of the people who live within a distance of five miles from the center of activity, which might be the village, a country school, or the home far from the village.

There was no activity that was restricted to invited guests. Whether it was a play-party at a home, the singing school, the literary, the "big meetin' " at the church, the molasses boiling, or whatever, it was always understood that everyone was welcome.

19

THE MOLASSES BOILING

One of the most enjoyable of the harvest time activities
that combined work with social activity was the making of sorghum, called the "molasses bilin'," which was held in the latter
part of September. Almost every farmer planted a good-sized
patch of cane in the late spring at corn-planting time. It was
planted in rows about three feet apart, which allowed room for
working between the rows. In late September the leaves were
stripped from the green stalks before the stalks were cut. Some
farmers cut the stalks before the leaves were stripped, leaving
the job of stripping to the women and girls.

One man went into the business of molasses making and
purchased the equipment for the molasses bilin' for as many as
a half dozen communities. It consisted of a mill with large rollers which pressed the juice from the stalks of cane, and an
evaporating pan in which the juice was boiled down to a thick
and sweet consistency, called molasses or sorghum. The man
who owned the equipment was an expert at making molasses,
who knew when the juice had been boiled to the correct consistency to make good molasses. A schedule was arranged
among farmers so that the molasses maker could take his equipment from place to place for all the farmers in the community.
Sometimes a farmer who did not have a large crop of cane
would cut his crop and haul it in a wagon to another farmers's
boiling, so that several farmers might have molasses boiled at
the same location.

The mill which pressed the juice from the cane was turned
by a single horse hitched to the end of a pole, which turned the
rollers of the mill as the horse walked around the mill in a circle.
The raw juice which flowed from the mill was poured into the
evaporating pan, which was heated by a wood-fire under it.
From one end of the long pan the juice was moved to the other
end as it cooked. The master-maker, who was in charge of the
entire operation, with a long-handled wooden paddle moved
the juice slowly through the sluices in the pan until it was ready

to be taken off through a spigot in the bottom of the pan. It was caught in buckets and poured into stone jars and jugs.

As the juice boiled and moved from one end of the pan to the other, a green scum rose to the top and was skimmed off and thrown in a hole which had been dug in the ground near the pan. This was called the "skimmin' hole."

Although the bilin' went on from morning till late at night, most of the people came at night, for that was when it became a "molasses bilin' party." An outside fire would be built to furnish light; and sometimes torches made of rags soaked in crude oil would be placed around the site. Young and old alike would make small spoon-like wooden paddles, dip them in the molasses as it neared the finishing end of the pan, and lick the warm, tasty, liquid from the paddles.

Some of the young men always got together and made plans to trick someone into stepping in the skimmin' hole; they carefully camouflaged it to fool their unsuspecting victim, who was almost always some young man who was trying to impress the young ladies. When he finally stepped in the skimmin' hole up to his knees and got the green skimmins on his breeches, he became the object of much teasing and laughter.

The young people played singing games, hide-and-seek, and other traditional games, while the older people tended to the molasses-making, with much pleasant conversation.

Such was the molasses "bilin'," one of the finest examples of communal work combined with much fun.

BEAN STRINGINGS AND APPLE PEELINGS

When green beans were ready to be prepared for canning or for pickling, or when apples had to be peeled and quartered for making apple butter, a party was given in the farmer's home, to which many people came to share the work and to enjoy the activities afterwards.

The participants in the bean stringing or apple peeling sat in a circle around a washtub, which received the strung beans or peeled and quartered apples. As the work went on, there was much conversation and sometimes story telling and singing. The young ladies would be getting things ready for the party which followed, making taffy so that it would be ready for the pulling, and preparing goodies to eat and cider to drink.

These work-and-play parties are a thing of the past now, but many elderly people will still remember that these parties helped fill their lives with happy experiences.

THE CORN-SHUCKIN'

Most farmers shucked their ripe corn after it had been cut and bound into fodder shocks in the field. But sometimes the corn was pulled from the stalks unshucked and brought to the barn, where it was placed in a large pile in the center of the barn floor. Then word was passed around that there was to be a corn-shuckin'. Men and women came to shuck the corn and to take part in the fun. When any man found a red ear of corn, he had the privilege of kissing the girl of his choice. Of course, if a married man found a red ear, he kissed his wife. This custom made it almost certain that no married man ever attended the corn-shuckin' without his wife.

The women prepared food and refreshments of fried chicken, pie, cake, and cider. These corn-shuckin' parties were always very popular, especially among the young people.

WHEAT-THRESHING TIME

Almost all farmers raised wheat, which was taken to the grist mill to be ground into flour for biscuits, light-bread, and flap jacks. Before the threshing machine came into use, grain had to be threshed by flailing. The wheat was placed in a large square box with low sides and beaten with a flail, which was a short stick attached by a leather strip to a long wooden handle.

The threshing machine was invented in 1834. The man who was able to own a threshing machine was kept busy through wheat harvest time going from farm to farm, threshing wheat for farmers in a wide region.

Farmers traded work at threshing time, for the help of ten or twelve men was needed. The work went on all day, and often it was dark when the men came to the farm home to eat a big meal. The meal was called supper, but today we would call it dinner. The three meals on the farm were breakfast, dinner, and supper. The word *lunch* referred only to a cold meal carried in a box or lunchbucket to be eaten at school or at fishing.

The wives of the workers combined their skills and efforts in preparing the meal for their men. There was no party after the meal was over, for the workers were always too tired. However, this communal activity was very important in helping to bring people together in a friendly relationship.

THE QUILTING BEE

The quilting bee was strictly a woman's work party, when the women of the community met at one of the homes to work on a quilt which was stretched on a frame. It was a small party, usually not more than a dozen women. Sometimes they made a "Friendship Quilt," made of different pieces brought to the party by the different women as an expression of their friendship. These quilting bees were important social gatherings for housewives, who exchanged ideas and knowledge about cooking, planting, cures, and other things important in their lives. Its nearest counterpart today is probably the bridge party.

THE "LITERARY"

By the beginning of this century the country school had become a center for community activities. The event that brought many people to the school on one night each month was called the "Literary." It was a meeting of all the pupils of the school, their parents and friends, who came to participate in such activities as debates, dramatic skits, readings, recitations, and spelling contests. Sometimes a team of pupils would debate against a team of adults on some popular subject. Spelling contests were popular, with pupils and adults participating. Choral singing was also an important part of the literary.

BOX SUPPERS AND PIE SOCIALS

Box suppers and pie socials were popular at the country school in the early years of this century. Their purpose was two-fold: to make money to purchase books for the school library and other necessary supplies for the school, and to provide an evening of fun for the people of the community. The ladies, young and old, prepared boxes of fine food to be auctioned off to the men at the schoolhouse on a night chosen for the social. The boxes were supposed to be wrapped in such a way that the owner's identity would not be known, but many girls would decorate their boxes with a special kind of bow or colored ribbon that would be recognized by the young men. That made the bidding highly competitive, for many a young man was willing to pay a high price to keep a rival from buying his girl's box.

At the pie social, pies were sold instead of boxes of food. Often the pie was sold by the "shadow-buying" method, with the girl standing behind a sheet so that the bidder could see only her dim shadow.

After the food was consumed, the big event was the cakewalk. The people would form a line and walk around the room in a circle singing a song. They had to walk under an upraised broom which was held by a person wearing a blindfold. When the song reached a certain specified word, the blindfolded person would let the broom fall, and the person whose head it touched was the winner of the cake. Traditional games were often played, such as "Old Dusty Miller," "Blind Man's Buff," and others.

THE SINGING SCHOOL

One of the most important events in the social and cultural life of the mountaineers was the beginning of the shape-note singing school. After the Civil War, the method of writing music in shaped notes was brought across the Allegheny Mountains from the Shenandoah Valley, where Harrisonburg, Virginia, had become the center for the printing of song books using this new American method. Itinerant teachers of this method came into West Virginia and taught "subscription schools," so-called because the teacher was paid for his services by voluntary subscriptions from families in the community where the school was taught. The teacher received a dollar a day and "boarded round" among various families. The school usually lasted from ten days to two weeks, during which time almost everyone in the community learned to read music and sing hymns in four-part harmony. People of all ages learned to read music, so that many communities became well known for their excellent singing.

After the singing teacher, whom we called the "singin' master," had moved on to teach in another community, the communal singing continued, with people meeting at one of the country churches on one night each week for what was always simply called "Singin'." Song books which had been purchased through the singin' master were kept in each home, and choral singing became an important activity in most homes. Singers used to come to our home on one night each week to sing, and we often went to other homes, where singing was the chief activity. When there was a funeral in the community, there was always a large choir to sing. When there was a wake for the dead, sometimes called a "settin'-up," a choir was there to sing the religious songs requested by the family. No accompaniment was ever used.

These traditions persisted in rural West Virginia until after the advent of radio, until television dealt the final blow to this aspect of rural life, and a new kind of singing was born, called "Country Music" and "Gospel Singing."*

The singing school, with the weekly singing that followed, was important also for its effect on the social life of the people. Many times I was told by couples, "We got married after we had started going together at the singing school." It served to bring people together and allowed them to express themselves as a group. Then, too, it had a significant effect on the religious life of the people, for the songs all expressed religious thoughts and feelings. Everybody sang, and no one expected to be entertained. Today, however, almost all the people at any gathering are listeners who are being entertained by a quartet, or at best, a small group of singing entertainers.

HALLOWEEN

Halloween is a combination of pagan and Christian practices. In the beginning of Christianity many pagan practices existed, some of which had religious significance. Some of these celebrations were adapted in time to Christian religious observances, but the non-religious parts of the celebrations

*For an explanation of shape-note singing, see Patrick W. Gainer, *Folk Songs from the West Virginia Hills* (Seneca Books, Grantsville, W.Va.), "Choral Singing in the Mountains."

were sometimes kept. This was true of the celebration that became known in Christianity as Hallowe'en, the evening of All-Saints Day. The word *hallow* comes from the Middle English *halwe*, meaning saint. November 1 is a holy day in the liturgical year of the Catholic Church, but it has no such significance to Protestants. Therefore, Catholics generally celebrated the evening before, or Halloween, with its non-religious, and sometimes evil, practices which had come down from paganism, and the following day they attended church for the veneration of the saints.

In rural West Virginia the chief feature of the celebration was the practice of playing the part of the evil spirits who came to earth on Halloween to bedevil mortals. After all, if a farmer's out-house was pushed over into the creek, it was the evil spirits who did it, thus providing an alibi for the young men who were the real culprits.

There were parties which people attended dressed in costumes and masks. "Dumb suppers" were set at which girls sat in silence at a table where a chair was left vacant for a lover to occupy. Traditional games were played, and it was not unusual for young people to play "kissing-games," such as "post office," "spin the bottle," and "pass the coin." "Trick or Treat" did not originate at Halloween until the third decade of this century. (See section on the Christmas celebration.)

CHRISTMAS

Among the Protestants living in the mountains in early days, and until the early years of this century, there was little celebration of Christmas. In England the Puritan influence caused Parliament to abolish the observance of saints' days and the "three grand festivals of Christmas, Easter, and Whitsuntide." The General Court of Massachusetts followed the example of the English Parliament in 1659, when it enacted that "anybody who is found observing, by abstinence from labor, feasting, or any other way, any such day as Christmas day, shall pay for every such offense five shillings." Christmas celebrations were regarded as Catholic, and thus looked upon with disfavor by Protestants generally.

Before electricity became common in every part of West Virginia, there were few house decorations, and not many people had Christmas trees. Children received few toys except those that were home-made. The village store sold firecrackers, toy cap pistols, and other noise-makers, so that Christmas became a day for much noise-making. In the early days of this century Christmas parties were sometimes given in the country schools on the last day of school before Christmas.

In later years, not long before the first World War, some communities set up a Christmas tree in one of the local churches or schoolhouse. People placed gifts on the tree for relatives and friends, and a local man wearing a Santa Claus costume took the gifts from the tree, reading the name of each recipient, who then was supposed to open the present before the whole gathering. The presents were frequently chosen to reveal something of the recipient's character, and often caused much loud laughter.

When people met on Christmas Day they greeted each other with the phrase, "Christmas Gift," and the one who spoke the greeting first was supposed to have good luck.

In the counties of West Virginia east of the Allegheny Mountains, Christmas was celebrated by "Belsnickling," a custom unknown in other parts of the state. This custom was brought into that part of the state by German people from Pennsylvania in the early part of the eighteenth century. The celebration started on Christmas eve, when a small group disguised in costumes and masks started out under the leadership of "Old Belsnickle" to visit the homes in the community. Each home had a candle in the window to guide the visitors.

Old Belsnickle would knock on the door, and the voice of the head of the family would ask fromwithin, "Who's there?"

"Old Belsnickle."

The voice inside the house would then invite, "Old Belsnickle, come in."

The door was then opened and all the visitors entered and lined up to be inspected by the members of the family, who tried to identify each visitor. Anyone who was correctly identified had to do a "trick," which meant a performance of some kind, such as a song, dance, or some clever act. If the persons in the company could not be identified, the whole group was treated to good things to eat and drink. Of course they were always treated, no matter what happened. As the group moved from one home to another, they would be joined by members of the last family visited, so that the group became larger as they moved from home to home.

This Christmas celebration was later adapted to the Halloween celebration in Jefferson County, West Virginia, and from there it quickly spread over the entire country. It was called "Trick or Treat," and still goes by that name. However, the original meaning of the word *trick* as some kind of performance soon changed to mean some kind of mischievous act.

WAKES

The word *wake* was originally *lyke-wake* or *liche-wake*, from the Anglo-Saxon *lic*, "a corpse," and *wake*, "to watch," "to keep vigil." It is an all-night watch of friends and relatives over the remains of the dead before the funeral. The custom is of unknown origin and antiquity. It was always observed in rural homes in the days before funeral parlors became common, and is sometimes still observed.

When a death occurred in the community, it was customary for friends to go immediately to the home to prepare the body for burial. At one time even the casket was made by someone in the community who was skilled at this kind of work. The relatives of the deceased were relieved of all expense if possible.

Friends brought food to the home in preparation for the wake, which might be held for more than one night if time were needed for relatives to arrive for the funeral. A choir was assembled for the singing of the old hymns that were appropriate for the occasion, and prayers were said. People often came for many miles to attend the wake. It was a solemn occasion, not a party. Alcoholic beverages were not served. It was a time when relatives of the deceased returned to the home place, and long-separated friends were re-united.

The old-world custom of tolling the bell when someone died was not usually observed in this part of the country. However, the bell of the church was always tolled as the funeral procession approached the church. This custom is almost never observed today.

PLAY PARTIES

A social gathering at which singing games were the chief activity was called a "play party." The games were traditional and singing was without any accompaniment. Popular among the games were "Old Dusty Miller," "Red Bird Through the Window," "Three in a Boat," and "Virginia Reel." "Kissing games," in which the prize was the privilege of kissing the person of your choice, such as "Post Office," "Spin the Bottle," "Guess Who," and many others, were part of the activities. Refreshments were always served, such as pie, cider, cake, candied popcorn, and taffy. "Taffy-pulling" was often a part of the activities.

In most homes square dancing was not permitted, for it was considered to be an activity suitable for the dance hall or for a barn-dance. There was usually singing at the play-party, the whole group singing together, and sometimes quartets and solos. The spirit of the play-party was one of informality, and many romances had their beginning at these parties.

Invitations were not given to these parties, but word was passed around that there would be a party at a certain home and everyone was welcome to come.

THE BIG MEETIN'

One of the most popular "gatherings" in rural West Virginia was the religious revival, called the "Big Meetin'." Its main purpose was, of course, to gain converts to Christianity, but its social significance was very great. It was an occasion for people to sing together, to hear preaching of the Word, and for young people to start romances. The denomination of the church where the Big Meetin' was held did not make much difference to most of the people who attended, for it was an occasion for people to be "saved," and they could then join the church of their choice, which was usually Methodist, Baptist, or United Brethren.

Word was passed around through the community that a Big Meetin' would begin at a certain church on a certain night. There was usually no definite time set for the termination of the Big Meetin', and sometimes when some people seemed to be on the verge of being saved but had not yet made the decision, the meeting would be prolonged as long as there was hope for the sinners. These undecided but hopeful ones were called "mourners," and a bench, called the "mourner's bench," was placed in the front of the church for the mourners. I have known certain young men who, wishing to have the meeting prolonged for their own social and romantic advancement, would come forth and sit on the mourner's bench.

The early rural churches always had two front doors. The females entered the church by the door on the left side and sat in the pews on that side of the church, while the males entered by the right-hand door and sat on that side. When the meeting ended each night, the young women would wait a little while to give the young men time to stand by the left-hand door to ask the girls, "May I see you home?" If a young lady refused a young man, it was said that "she gave him the mitten."

The singing of old hymns was an enjoyable and rewarding experience at the "Big Meetin'." The singing was always without accompaniment, and everyone took part in it. There is a misconception among some people that there was much clapping of hands and stamping of feet when the songs were sung. Sometimes a woman among the congregation, rarely a man, would come to the front of the church to "shout," which was really a kind of dance or movement from one side of the church to the other while singing a song.

SERENADE FOR NEWLYWEDS

When a couple got married, it was the custom to give them a serenade on their first night together. In some parts of the region it was called a "shivaree." People would gather at night outside the house where the couple were spending the night; and there would be much noise-making: beating on drums or tin pans, or by blowing home-made whistles, or shooting guns in the air. Sometimes there was singing.

The bridegroom was sometimes taken taken away from the house on a rail, and on rare occasions he might be thrown in the creek. It was all done in fun, and the bridegroom was not supposed to become angry, even though he might be treated somewhat roughly.

THE INFARE

The word *infare* comes from Old English: *in* plus *faran,* to go in. It was a reception held in the home of the newly-married couple. Word was "spread around;" no invitations were issued, but people in the community knew that they were invited. Refreshments were served and games were played very much as at the play-party. Neighbors often brought gifts of food and other things to be used in the home of the newly-wed couple.

THE PARTY LINE

In the early years of this century in most rural communities in West Virginia, the telephone party line was a very important factor in affording a means of communication among people, where homes were often separated by great distances. Country living did not afford "back-yard" conversation between neighbors.

Most communities were served by local telephone companies which were owned and operated by the home owners of a wide-spread community. Each home could have a telephone by purchasing a share in the company for a small yearly fee. A switchboard was purchased and placed in a small building or in someone's home, where a person served as operator for a small salary. Numerous party lines were run into the central switchboard, which was simply called "central," where the operator could connect the lines together.

If one wished to call a party on his own line, he simply turned the crank on his telephone on the wall to ring that party. If he wished to talk to someone on another line, he rang one long ring, and "Central" would answer with a short ring. Usually the central operator would recognize the voice of the caller. There were no numbers, and telephones were identified only by names. The caller would likely say, "Mary, give me John Smith's," or "Mary, I want to talk to Sally."

On some lines there were as many as a dozen telephones. Anyone on the line could listen to the conversation of others, and this was generally expected. Sometimes one could hear several people—usually women—exchanging recipes and cures for common ailments. Six short rings meant an emergency, and when anyone heard this ring he hurried to the telephone to learn what was needed. People who could sing or play instruments were often requested to perform with the receiver "off the hook" so that people could listen. On Sundays when the central switchboard was not operating, the lines would all be connected so that the listening audience was widespread. Thus, broadcasting by wire was current long before it became common by radio.

"Uncle" Bud O'Dell, of Nicholas County, whose favorite song was "My Old Hickory Cane," told me that he was often asked to sing that song over the telephone. Word would be spread about that Uncle Bud was going to sing, so that there would be numerous listeners. The music emanating from one telephone did not disrupt the service from another telephone on the line. It was not unusual for two persons to carry on a conversation while music was coming from a third telephone on the line.

Ghostlore
❖❖❖❖❖❖❖❖❖❖

Of the numerous tales that I have found in the oral traditions of the people of the West Virginia hills, many tell of people's experiences with ghosts or spirits. However, we must not make the mistake of classifying a tale as a folk tale merely because it has something to do with some kind of occult phenomena. It becomes a folk tale only when it has become a part of oral tradition and has so existed for at least several generations. It must be preserved in oral tradition and transmitted from one generation to another orally. Thus it changes in time, re-touched by the imagination of each story teller, and it takes on something of the personality of each narrator.

The belief in ghosts is, of course, universal among the people of the world. Man seeks contact with the spiritual world, and is quick to attribute a spiritual origin to any phenomena which he cannot readily understand. If he hears a strange and mysterious sound which he cannot identify, he is willing to believe that it is a spiritual manifestation. If he sees some mysterious object, such as the will-of-the-wisp, which is natural, he believes it to be a spirit. People *want* to believe in ghosts. Professional quacks make fortunes from gullible people who believe that these quacks can bring back the voices of loved ones or friends who have departed from this world.

Most ghosts who appear in folk tales are really revenants—

unlaid ghosts, who have remained on earth to give a message to the living. As a rule, these ghosts are the spirits of people who have met violent deaths at the hands of murderers, and they wish to disclose the identity of the murderer. These ghosts usually remain on earth until some wrong is corrected.

Ghosts usually appear in the same form as the humans they were before death. Sometimes the living person who meets one of these revenants does not recognize the ghost as such, but thinks it is a living person. For example, in "The Suffolk Miracle," an old-world ballad which still survives in West Virginia, the girl does not realize she is seeing the ghost of her lover who has been dead for twelve months; when he comes for her on horseback to take her back home, she willingly rides on the horse behind him. When he complains of a headache, she ties her handkerchief around his head. When they arrive at her home, her lover disappears, but when they open his grave they find the corpse with the handkerchief tied around his head. In the ballad, "The Wife of Usher's Well," a mother's three sons, who have been absent for a long time, return to her in the night. She invites them to eat and drink, but they tell her they must go back. It is then that she becomes aware that these are the ghosts of her sons who have come back to stop her tears which have wet their winding sheets.

Ghosts have appeared in some of the world's greatest literature. In *Hamlet* and in *Macbeth* Shakespeare brought ghosts upon the stage to appear before a credulous audience. Christopher Marlowe, in *The Tragical History of Doctor Faustus,* brought on the stage the ghost of Helen of Troy as the most beautiful woman who ever lived, and Doctor Faustus kisses her passionately before the audience. The poet Shelley, in *Hymn to Intellectual Beauty,* writes, "While yet a boy I sought for ghosts in many a listening cave and ruin." It is said that the famous Samuel Johnson searched for ghosts in London.

Almost without exception, the people who told ghost tales to me believed in their actual existence. A common preface to a tale is the statement: "Now this really happened." I think one could safely say that most of the ghost stories did originate in actual happenings. People sometimes ask me, "Do you really believe in ghosts?" My answer is that there are many mysteries which cannot be explained. The stories which we have included in this book have no other purpose than to entertain. Therefore, we suggest that the reader suspend his disbelief in ghosts for a brief time and enjoy the stories.

JIM BARTON'S FIDDLE

"Jim Barton's Fiddle" is a good example of a story that has its origin in fact, but time has turned it into a folktale which has been retouched by the imagination of each narrator for several generations. Note how the narrator of this story supplies colorful details, supporting his statement with, "They say." Folk tales, like folk songs, are oral literature and should be heard rather than read. The personality of the narrator is an important part of the folk tale. Therefore, I have tried to convey to the reader something of the character of the narrator of each story, whenever possible.

It was a warm night in early fall, when our "hired-man," whose name was Othe, and I were out on the ridge listening to the dogs chase a fox, when we passed by the old Barton place. Neither of us had a watch with us that night, but we knew by the crowing of the roosters in the valleys on either side of us that it was midnight. There was a little clearing just before we got to the Barton place. We sat down on a log and looked toward the old log house, which had fallen pretty much into ruin. The roof had sunk in, but part of the walls still stood, and even the front door and one window looked much as they must have looked many years ago. The paling fence was weighed down by climbing roses, and two large cedar trees stood in front, one on either side of the gate. The moon was full that night, and we could see things pretty well.

I liked the hired man, because he had such a gentle way of telling about little things that made them seem important. He had not had much formal schooling, but in his heart he was a poet. He had a feeling for nature that was Wordsworthian. He even felt that there was life in inanimate things—like the time he told me how he felt when he was picking rocks up in the meadow and he found them sometimes in little clusters like families. He said it seemed just like a mother with a lot of little ones around her, and he hated to separate them.

We had just sat down on the log when we heard the roosters crowing. The big cedar trees were throwing shadows across the front of the old Barton house. Suddenly I was aware of a strange sound which seemed to be coming from the ruins of the old house. It sounded like a fiddle playing softly, and I could have sworn that it was an old tune which I had often heard my grandfather whistle, an old fiddle tune called "The Devil's Quickstep." I could see that the hired man heard it too, for he looked at me and smiled, but he said nothing for a few minutes. Then he said, "Well, son, you've just heard Jim Barton's fiddle."

"But there's no one living there," I said.

"No, not now," he said. And I knew by the way he settled himself on the log that he was going to tell me a story. He had a way of fixing his mouth in a kind of pucker as he looked up, as if reading something from a wall.

"I reckon you never heard of the Bartons and what happened to them here in this old house, did you?"

I had to admit that I had never heard much but some bits of stories and rumors about this old place, but I had always wanted to hear more about it. He then began his story:

Well, it was a long time ago that the Bartons lived here. There was three of them—old Peter, his wife Sarry, and their boy Jim. When I was a boy I used to pass here and see old Aunt Sarry a-putterin' around the yard, and she always wanted me to stop so she could give me somethin'—an apple or some cookies. I was afraid then, 'cause she lived out here by herself and lots of folks said they's pretty sure that queer things went on here. That was their way of hintin' that maybe Aunt Sarry was a witch. But no one ever said she did any harm to anybody. Some said they could hear sounds like a fiddle playin' in the night.

Aunt Sarry was from a family of fiddle players. They say there was never a one of them that couldn't play a fiddle. Even the girls could play just about as good a fiddle as the men.

Peter Barton was such a strait-laced young feller that it's a wonder that he ever went out to Sarry's place, but Sarry was such a pretty girl that Peter couldn't stay away. For that matter, they say there was a lot of other young men that went there because of Sarry, but Peter was the one that got her.

Peter Barton thought the fiddle was the instrument of the devil, but that's the way he'd been raised. Some said he always wanted to go into preachin', but he had to work so hard to make a livin' that he never had time to practice at preachin'. He could make a powerful prayer, though, and lots of folks went to meetin' just to hear Peter Barton make a prayer.

Peter built this house himself and had it all ready for him and Sarry when they got married. Oh, she had come here a few times before they got married and brought some roses from the home place so it wouldn't look so bare when they moved in. When they had the infare, Sarry's pappy and some of the boys came to see how she was fixed, but they knowed better than to fetch ary fiddle here.

Well, it was only a year till the boy was born, and they named him James. They say Peter wanted to call the boy after one of the prophets in the Old Testament, but Sarry wanted to call him James because that was the name of the grandpappy she liked so much. But she told Peter she thought it would be nice to call him after one of the apostles, just like he was, only if they called him Peter, folks would be a-mixin' them up. So he agreed that James was a good name.

I reckon they was right happy, but some say that Peter blamed Sarry because she couldn't have any more children. And he never liked to take her and Jim over to her pappy's place, for he was afraid they might hear the fiddle and take a likin' to it. They say Peter was powerful religious. Some said they passed here at supper time and they could hear Peter sayin' the blessin' long before they got this far. He'd begin awful loud and then get soft-like as he went along, till when he got to the *amen* you could hardly hear him. And he never missed takin' Sarry and the boy over to church of a Sunday to meetin' —and the preacher always called on him to pray.

But they say Peter was a hard man to deal with when it come to tradin'. I reckon it was because he'd always had to work so hard for what he got. They say he didn't trust people much, and people generally didn't care much for him as a person.

One day Sarry's ma was a-ailin' and they sent for Sarry to come. Peter took her and the boy over on the mules—he always had a pair of mules—and while they was there Jim noticed the fiddle a-hangin' on the wall, and he asked about it. His grandpap took it down and played a few tunes for him. They say Peter was fit to be tied, but it made Sarry's ma feel better. When they got away from there, Peter laid the law down to Sarry and Jim. Jim was a right smart chunk of a boy then. Peter said that he never wanted Jim to touch a fiddle, and if he ever took to the fiddle, he couldn't live in the same house with him. They say that both Jim and his ma was afraid of Peter, for Peter was a strong-tempered man.

One way Peter had of makin' money was to run a raft of logs down the river. In them days there was a lot of timber in this country, and it was cut and put in the river to be made into rafts and floated down the river when it got up high enough. Not many men wanted to take a raft down, but Peter was always tryin' to get enough money to buy more land, so he'd take a raft down the river every chance he got. It took about four days to take a raft down and get back, because he had to get back on foot.

One day when Peter was away, one of Sarry's brothers fetched Sarry and Jim over to see her ma, because she was a-ailin' again. Jim's grandpap played the fiddle again for him, and they say the boy liked it so much that the old man told him to take it home with him. Sarry said she was afraid, because Peter would never allow a fiddle in the house. "Well," the old man says, "Why don't you take it back and let Jim learn to play it while his pappy is away? And just before Peter comes back you can hide it in the loft." The boy was so tickled at the idea that Sarry finally gave in, and they took the fiddle back with them.

Well, them two must have had a time together when Peter was away from home. Fiddlin' was in Jim's blood, and I reckon his ma learned him a lot of tunes.

One night after it had rained a couple of days, Peter said he would go down the river the next day, for there was a sizeable raft ready, and he 'lowed the river was about right. The next morning he left right early, and said he aimed to get back on the fourth day after that. It might take a little longer if it rained more, for some of the small streams would be up, making it hard to get back on foot.

Sarry and Jim waited till late that afternoon before they dared get the fiddle down from the loft. Finally Jim got it down and played one tune after another while his ma sat in that old rockin' chair that her pa had give her, and she just listened. Maybe she took the fiddle herself now and then and played a few tunes. Anyway, they must have been havin' a good time of it.

Well, Peter went down the river, but when he got down about ten miles where the river makes a bend and narries down where there's some big rocks, his raft commenced to break apart. They say he was mighty lucky to get out of the river alive, for the raft went all to pieces. There was nothin' for him to do but come on back home. He stopped at a house and dried himself, and it was well after dark when he got back on the ridge where he lived here in this house. He 'lowed it was time Sarry and Jim would be asleep. But when he got a little piece from his house he could see the lamp a-burnin'. I reckon he was about where we're a-settin' now when he heard the fiddle a-playin'.

Well, It's hard to tell just what kind of thoughts come into the mind of Peter Barton right at that moment. I've heard Uncle Dave Linger tell the story, and he said he'd heard *that* part of it from Peter himself. But Uncle Dave was never one to care much for fiddle playin', and most likely he sided with Peter. He said Peter told him how he got down on his knees right there inside the yard and asked the Lord to help him do the right thing. But I've heard Uncle Jim Danley tell the story, too, just the way Aunt Sarry told it to Uncle Jim's wife. Peter opened the door and walked slow-like into the room without sayin' a word. Then he took the fiddle out of the boy's hands, and he took his knife and cut all four strings. He took that fiddle and hung it on a nail just to the left of the fireboard where Aunt Sarry kept her hussif when she was a-doin' needle work. Then Peter turned and spoke: "There hangs the instrument of the devil. I would a-broke it in a hundred pieces, but I want it to hang there as a lesson to all them who will not obey. I have said that my son could not live in this house if he ever brought such an instrument under this roof. Now let him go to his grandpappy's and see if he has another fiddle. Let him go *now*, and let him stay there."

Well, Sarry tried to take the blame, but Peter wouldn't listen. It was dark and Jim had no light, but he wasn't a-carin', the way he felt. He didn't take a thing with him but his coat and hat, and he left right then. Sarry 'lowed he'd go to her Pa's place, and when Peter cooled off, Jim would come back.

It was early next mornin' when Peter went out to fetch the cow to milk, that he found Jim's body. He was a-layin' at the foot of that cliff yonder, where he'd fell over and broke his neck when his head hit a stump. Peter picked Jim's body up and carried it to the house.

Peter and Sarry Barton went on a-livin' here in this house after that. They say Peter changed a lot. He never went down the river on a raft again, and he stayed around the house most of the time. He and Sarry went to church most every Sunday when there was preachin', but Peter never said the prayer he used to. Some said he asked the preacher never to call on him again.

The fiddle with its strings cut hung on that wall, and I reckon no one ever touched it. It was four years after Jim died that Peter got killed. He'd gone down to the barn to hitch up the mules, and Aunt Sarry heard him a-rarin' at one of them. After a while she didn't hear him any more, and she got worried that somethin' had happened to him. She went down to the barn and found him with his head split open where the mule had kicked him.

Of course, folks talk a lot when things like that happen, and most of them don't know the true story at all. Some of them said that Peter had said that he would live only four years after what had happened in his house—one year for each of the cut fiddle strings. Anyhow, that's the way it turned out. They buried him out there in the graveyard along side of Jim.

After that Aunt Sarry lived here by herself. One of her brothers wanted her to come back to the old home place to live after their pa had died, but she just wouldn't leave this place. Folks that lived over this hill used to go out of their way to pass this place so's to stop and see Aunt Sarry. She lived here by herself for about twenty years, and it was then that some folks began to say that queer things was a-goin' on at night. More than one passed here late at night comin' from singin' or preachin', and said they heard a sound like a fiddle a-playin'. It might have been the wind a-blowin' in them cedar trees, that had got pretty big by then.

As I said, I used to come past here in the daytime when I was just a boy, and Aunt Sarry was pretty old then. She'd always give me something to eat—an apple or a cookie, and sometimes a piece of pie. I saw the fiddle a-hangin' there, but I'd been told never to say anything about it, and she didn't seem to notice it.

Well, it was one Saturday mornin' that some folks was a-goin' past here, and they stopped to see how Aunt Sarry was. They called, but Aunt Sarry didn't answer; and so they walked up to the house and opened the door. There they found Aunt Sarry a-settin' in her old rockin' chair and a-holdin' that fiddle in her lap. She had a smile on her face, but her eyes was closed just like she was asleep. But when they went over to her, they found she was dead. They said they never saw a person look so peaceful and natural-like as Aunt Sarry in that chair.

Well, that's all there is to the story. They buried Aunt Sarry Barton out there on the other side of Jim, so that Jim was a-restin' between her and Peter. No one ever lived in this house after that. Some say that Jim Barton's fiddle can be heard yet on some nights just about midnight.

THE GHOST OF MRS. GREEN

One of the dearest souls it was my privilege to meet during the many years that I collected folklore in the hills of West Virginia was "Aunt" Mattie Long, who lived in Gassaway, Braxton County. Aunt Mattie was eighty-two years old when I first went to her home in the summer of 1952 to hear her sing and tell stories. Her voice was very clear, and her outlook on life was one of optimism and great religious faith. For her, the borderline between the spiritual world and the world of reality was a very thin one, and she felt that now and then some sight of the spiritual was revealed to man, either through what we call miracles, or through God's permission to a spirit to return to the earth to correct some wrong that had been committed.

Aunt Mattie's great-grandfather had come from Scotland before the Revolutionary War and had fought in that war. Her father was a soldier in the Union Army in the Civil War. Aunt Mattie's husband was no longer living, but they had lived a happy married life for sixty years.

My uncle used to tell me about a woman named Mrs. Green on a place on Steer Creek. She had several children, but she never was married. Late one night when she and her children were all asleep, someone came in the house and killed her.

The children hadn't heard a thing in the night and didn't know anything had happened till the next morning when they found their mother murdered.

Well, some people whispered around that the murderer was a certain married man, and Mrs. Green threatened to tell his wife that he'd been seeing her, and he killed her to keep her from telling his wife. Anyhow, the sheriff claimed he tried to get some evidence, but they never arrested anybody. After that they could see Mrs. Green walking around the field on John Perkins' farm, where she had lived in a small house that she had rented from him. No doubt she was trying to find somebody who would listen to her so she could tell who the guilty person was. But the people who saw her said they were afraid and would run when they saw her walking around in the field. People are like that. If anyone would have asked her, "In God's name, what do you want?" she might have told who the guilty person was. After a few years no one ever saw the ghost any more.

THE WOMAN WHO CAME CRYING

A story that Aunt Mattie Long liked to tell was about the woman who came crying, for her Uncle Archie was very much a part of this story, and Aunt Mattie had heard it many times. Her eyes brightened, and her voice became stronger as she began her story.

I had an uncle named Archie Armstrong, who married a girl named Dean. They lived on a hill above Birch River some years ago. Uncle Archie's wife was my father's sister. Well, a woman would come up around the house crying. The women would see the woman a-crying, and so would Uncle Archie's boy, Chaney. But it had never come to Uncle Archie—he'd never seen it. One day the baby got sick, and they wanted an onion to make a poultice to put on it. The girls were afraid to go to the garden to get the onion, for they were afraid they might see that woman who came crying. Chaney said, "Come on, I'll go. And if I see the thing, I'll knock it down." And he went out with the girls to get the onion, and here came that thing right up in their face, that woman who was crying. The girls got scared and broke to run. One of them got in the house, and the other one got on the porch and fainted. And Chaney stood there and fought that thing till he got clear back to the house. But he said he couldn't hit anything. He said it was right there crying and making a noise, but he said there wasn't a thing there when he'd strike with his fist.

One night after that, some of them went out on the porch. And this woman came up there a-crying, up next to the porch. And they called, "Now, Archie, come out here and see it. It's right here in the yard." So he got up and went out to the porch, and there it was—that woman standing there a-crying. And he watched that a little bit, turned right around, went back into the house, and fell across the bed. And they never got him out of that bed that night. The next morning he got up and began tearing his house down. And he tore his house down and moved it down on to Birch River.

THE PASSING SOUL

Aunt Mattie often waited on people when they were sick, and she was a midwife for many years. When a woman in the community died, Aunt Mattie would go to the home to help prepare the body for burial. For, as Aunt Mattie said to me, "They didn't have any funeral homes in those days." One experience she told me about illustrates her great faith in the efficacy of prayer.

I went over there that night to wait on that woman. She'd died of a fever. I washed her and dressed her, and her

body was put in the coffin, which was in the parlor. I was standing there by the coffin. They had taken the lamp to the other
room and put it on the fireboard there, so it was almost dark in
the parlor. But that didn't scare me. All at once I looked out the
window, and I saw a white thing about a foot square, turning
around as it passed the door. I couldn't tell what it was, for I'd
never seen anything like it before. So I said, "Lord, show it to
me again." And that thing came right back, moving and turning. But still I couldn't tell what it was. So I said, "Lord, show
it to me again, show it to me the third time." And it came back
again, just like the Lord was answering me. But still I couldn't
tell what it was, and I didn't see it any more. They say that
sometimes the passing soul can be seen before it takes flight for
heaven, and no doubt that is what I saw.

THE GHOST OF THE JILTED GIRL

*One day in 1958 I visited Elliot Johnson in his home in
Logan County. He had worked hard in the coal mines for many
years. His voice was soft and mellow, and his eyes brightened
as he told me of a frightful experience he had with a ghost.*

I had a ghost to haunt me once. She was a sweetheart
of mine, but I didn't marry her. She wanted me to marry her.
And after I married another girl, this sweetheart took poison
and killed herself. And she haunted me so that I had to leave
that house and come up here to live. She'd grab me in the bed.
The first time, she caught the sheet, grabbed it and pulled it. I
woke up and tried to hold the sheet, but she pulled it out of my
hand. I said, "Oh, imagination! I'm going to stay here in the
house anyhow." It wouldn't come *every* night, but every *other*
night. One night it came and caught me right here up under
the throat and back of the neck. Brother, she had a vise on me,
and it looked like I couldn't get away at all. Finally, I ran in and

got loose. Well, that night I said, "I think I'll go upstairs, for I don't believe it will bother me there." I went upstairs, and someone says, 'Boy, did you come up?' I said, "Yeah, I got lonesome down there." Well, the next night after that she came upstairs, but she didn't bother me. I heard the footsteps coming up the stairs, "Pit, pit, pit"—coming right up the stairs. I turned the light on quick, but I didn't see nothing, but she took all my clothes and I heard a sound like *woo*. . . . And I said, "All right." I went down the next morning a little before day, and she went down stairs. It sounded like someone rolling marbles down the stairs "bub, bub, bub, bub, bub." So, I figgered I'd get out of there. She couldn't come across a stream of water. So I moved up here, and she ain't bothered me any more since.

THE VENGEFUL GHOST
OF THE MURDERED GIRL

One summer afternoon in 1958, I sat with Bird Cook on the porch of his home on Horse Creek, Raleigh County, as he told me the story of the girl who was murdered by her rival in love, and how the ghost of the murdered girl remained on earth until she got revenge. The story is told in Mr. Cook's own language.

One time there was two girls lived in our neighborhood. One of 'em was my aunt and one was a Gunnoe girl. And they got to talkin' to a boy, and this Gunnoe girl was a-gettin' the best of the Cook girl. That was my aunt, you know. So my aunt just fixed up a little bit of chicken and dumplins and took it over to her sister's house where this Gunnoe girl was a-stayin', and told the balance of the family not to eat none of that chicken and dumplins. Well, this Gunnoe girl, she eat a bit of it. In about five or six hours she commenced a-gettin' sick. And she got to vomit-in' and throwin' up—you never seen anybody get as sick as she did—and in about three days she died. Well, they had a big trial over it. The courts was pretty scarce then. We just had a justice of the peace court out on the hill where we lived. And so they lawed around there about that, and this man, whose name was Everett Wiley, a boy from this country, he was a witness in it. When this Gunnoe girl died, Wiley quit the Cook girl and had nothing to do with her.

So this Cook girl married another feller a short time after that. And this here girl she'd killed, the Gunnoe girl, why she'd come of a night, git on her and choke her, choke her prin nearly to death. You never heered such a time they had. She couldn't see nothing, but she'd just choke the life out of her, and her man couldn't sleep with her on account of it. Then this Cook girl married another feller, and she couldn't stay with him either.

Later on, my brother moved in this house where the woman lived, where the poison was taken in. But before he moved in, me and him went there one night together. We intended to keep batch for a time. The first night we built up a big fire in the house. We didn't have no light, just a pine torch or something like that. Way in the night we was just dozin' off to sleep when somethin' hit the side of the house . . . "Boom!" We had a big pile of wood piled up by the fireplace, and that just scattered all over the floor. Well, it sceered the life out of us, and we didn't know what to think. My brother says to me, "What will we do?" I says, "Let's git out of here." I would never go back to that house after that.

But he got married and him and his wife moved in there. And that would come in all kinds of forms. When there was a big snow on the ground it would come just like cows walkin'—you've heered cattle walkin' through the snow and their feet a-screekin' under the snow. He'd think the cows got in the lot, and he'd go out there to put 'em out and couldn't see a track or nothin'. There'd come a sound like they'd poured a bushel of walnuts on the house, and he'd hear 'em roll off and hit the ground around the house. He'd go out there and couldn't see a thing in the world. Now, it would come in all kinds of shapes, you know. He could hear a sound in the kitchen like a person vomiting. And it got so that he couldn't sleep and couldn't enjoy life. And that house got burned up, and he never did hear tell of it any more. Nobody knows what started the fire, but I believe it was just so willed to be. It was a pretty bad tale, if you get the whole details of it. When two girls fall out over a man, and one poisons the other'n, you know that's pretty bad. I believe it would be a good lesson to have that published. It would teach the young girls not to do things like that.

THE GHOST OF THE PEDDLER ON THIRD RUN

The story of the ghost of the murdered peddler is known in many parts of America, and West Virginia traditional lore preserves several stories of this kind. There was a time, before good roads became a reality, that peddlers often traveled through rural sections, selling a variety of wares to country people. These peddlers of necessity carried substantial sums of cash with them. They would often seek overnight lodging in the homes of farmers, where they received good food and lodging for themselves and for their horses that pulled the wagon.

One story of the peddler's ghost comes from Gilmer County, on Third Run of the Little Kanawha River, about two miles from my boyhood home. My grandfather told it to me.

A peddler stopped one night at a farmhouse on Third Run, a short distance from the river. The peddler was never seen after that night, and the story quickly spread about that the head of the family killed him in the night by cutting off his head with a corn cutter. According to the story, the peddler's head was buried under an apple tree not far from the house. The body was weighted with chains and thrown in a deep hole in the river. After that, the headless ghost of the peddler was seen by several people. Mr. Hinzman, who was well known for his sobriety and truthfulness, told me how one dark night when he was driving through the woods in his farm wagon past the place where the peddler was murdered, the headless ghost of the peddler got in the wagon seat beside him and rode to the edge of the woods with him. At the edge of the woods the ghost just disappeared. After that, the ghost of the peddler was not seen again.

THE COLLINS BETTS PEDDLER

Grandfather told of another peddler's ghost that was seen near Grantsville, in Calhoun County.

It is said that a peddler stopped one night at the home of Collins Betts. That night the peddler must have been murdered, for he was not seen again. It is said that there was a blood stain on the floor of one of the rooms, and the stain could not be removed. Even to this day, they say, there is a stain on the floor. Many people reported seeing and hearing the ghost of the peddler, who no doubt was trying to inform some one among the living of the secret of his death.

THE CRYING INFANT

Gale Miller, a teacher in a rural school in Gilmer County and a student in my class in folklore at Glenville State College, told me the story of the crying infant, which he had heard from his father. Gale lived near the haunted house.

In Gilmer County there is an old house in which many years ago there lived a couple with two very pretty daughters. The girls were often escorted home from singing or preaching by handsome young men of the community. Then the younger of the girls was not seen in public for some time, and word soon spread that they were expecting the bees to swarm at this house. (To expect the bees to swarm meant that a baby was expected.) After a period of almost a year, the girl again appeared at church with the other members of the family. The explanation for her absence was that she had been living with relatives in another part of the state.

Years later, after this family had moved away, a young couple came to live in the house. Each night the mysterious crying of a baby could be heard coming from beneath the hearthstone of the fireplace. Thinking the sound might be caused by an air current under the stone, they lifted the hearthstone and found the bones of a tiny infant. They took the bones and buried them in the graveyard. The crying of the infant was not heard after that.

THE HEADLESS HORSEMAN
OF POWELL MOUNTAIN

This story is well known among the people who live in and around Birch River, a village at the foot of Powell Mountain in Nicholas County. In recent years the road over the mountain has been relocated and modernized, and the ghost of the headless horseman is seen no more.

The story was told to me by Sylvia Cox, a student in my class at Glenville State College.

Out on the top of Powell Mountain in Nicholas County there is a lonely grave. It is the final resting place of Henry Young, a young man who was killed by the "home guard" during the Civil War. During the Civil War civilians sometimes organized into groups who called themselves the "Home Guard." Their purpose was supposed to be to protect their homes against the ravages of enemy soldiers, but some of them were in reality nothing more than guerilla bands of outlaws. It was such a group that murdered Henry Young.

A lonely road, now seldom used, winds down the hill from the grave. Part way down the hill there is a huge rock, which in days of old made a fine camping spot for people who came from miles away to gather chestnuts in the fall. Every night, about midnight, Henry Young rides that road. First can be heard the clanking of chains which bound him, then as the shadowy outline of horse and rider come into view, one notices that the rider has no head. Closer they come, and out of the night emerges the headless horseman, carrying his head in his lap. He does not stop, and he bothers no one. He does not even so much as move the head in his lap to right or left, but he passes on down the trail to emerge again the following night just at midnight.

THE SHUE MURDER CASE

Priscilla Jones, a teacher in Greenbrier County, West Virginia, told the story of the Shue murder case. She said she had put the story together from the accounts she had heard from several people who had lived in the county all their lives.

Young Mrs. Shue died suddenly from what was diagnosed as a heart attack. Not long after the young woman's burial, her mother was in bed one night when her daughter came to her and said that she had been murdered by her husband. She told her mother that her neck had been broken. The mother informed the sheriff of her experience and insisted that her daughter's body be exhumed and examined for a broken neck. The sheriff insisted that it was only a dream which the mother had, but finally the mother succeeded in having the body of her daughter exhumed. They discovered that her neck had really been broken. The husband was tried for the murder and convicted. The records show that the husband was sentenced to prison for life, and he died in prison.

THE TRAGIC STORY OF ELLEN AND EDWARD

Mrs. Nina Propst, of Pendleton County, contributed this story which came down to her through family tradition.

Lon Bartlett stood on the porch of his house and looked out over the hills, where he saw the full moon rising above the horizon. After watching the full moon for a few minutes, now shining through the oak trees on the distant ridge, he called to his wife, who was in the kitchen waiting for a cake to bake.

"Lila, come out here and see the moon. I want to know if you see the same thing I see."

"What is it, Lon?" she asked as she came through the door.

"Look yonder on the ridge, Lila. What do you see?"

"It's a woman, Lon! She's running along the ridge toward the cove. Look at her long hair and her long white dress. Listen, Lon, there is the scream!"

Across the valley came a shrill scream, like the wail of a woman in terrible agony. Along the ridge she moved, screaming, and it looked as if the moon must be shining through her body. Then she passed out of sight over the end of the ridge, but still the shrill wail echoed in the valley for several minutes.

"Well, Lila, this is the third time we've seen her since we moved here. It's been three months now, and we've seen her each month just when the moon is full. I don't know what it is, but I am going to try to find out. I never did believe in ghosts, but I think we've seen one." The Bartletts were a young couple who had recently moved into this small house in the country about two miles from the small town, where Lon worked in a store. They hadn't said anything to anyone about what they had seen, for they didn't think anyone would believe them.

There was an old lady named Mrs. Sims, who lived not far from the young couple. She lived by herself in a little house just down the road in a small clearing. They decided they would go to her the next day, which was Sunday, to ask her if she knew anything about what they had seen. It was a warm afternoon when they went to see Mrs. Sims, who was sitting alone on her porch. She appeared to be at least ninety, but she could hear well, and her voice was clear as she welcomed them. Together they told her what they had seen and heard each month when the moon was full.

"We don't want you to think we are making up a story, Mrs. Sims. We both saw the same thing, and we heard the screams. Have you ever heard anything about it?"

"Yes, I've heard it," said Mrs. Sims. She paused as if trying to decide whether or not to say more. Then she began to tell the story as the young couple listened in silence.

"When I was a little girl my father used to tell me the story. He knew the people who used to live in the house that stood on the ridge yonder. The house caught fire one night long after anybody quit living in it, and it burned to the ground before they could put the fire out. But a long time ago there was a big family lived there. They had seven sons and just the one daughter, who was the youngest of the family. They say the boys were pretty rough and got into a lot of fights, but they all just worshiped that little sister, whose name was Ellen. When she got to be about seventeen they say she was the prettiest thing ever lived, with her blue eyes and her long golden hair. Her brothers would never let any fellow touch her, nor hardly even look at her.

"On her eighteenth birthday they had a big play-party for her. They used to have play-parties around here, and they'd play the old singing games. They didn't send out invitations then as they do now. The word just got around, and everybody was welcome to come, and generally a lot of people did come.

"There was a young fellow who had just come to this community from some other place. He was a carpenter, and had built a lot of houses for people over in the next county at the county seat. Well, this young fellow showed up at the party, and they say he couldn't take his eyes off that girl. The brothers didn't like it, but she was getting to be pretty much her own boss by then. After that the young man came to the house quite often, and he and the girl would sit in the parlor, but one or two of the boys would always be with them.

"One day the boys all got together to go deer hunting, and they asked the young man—I can't remember his last name, but his first name was Edward—they asked him to meet them at the head of the hollow in the cove, and they'd see that he got a deer. They said they had seen a big buck with several doe there in the cove, and since the young man had never been deer hunting, they'd let him have the first shot when they saw a deer. They told him to bring a stout rope along so they could tie the deer up and carry it home.

"When Edward told Ellen that he was going deer hunting with her brothers, she was against it. She said she was afraid for him, with so many men and all with guns, and he had no experience with guns. But Edward said it would be a good chance for him to get in good with her brothers, so he wanted to go.

"That evening the brothers all came in and said that Edward had not showed up in the cove. They reckoned that he had changed his mind about hunting, but didn't have a chance to let them know. That night, about the middle of the night, Ellen woke up screaming, and said she dreamed that Edward came to her and said he'd been killed. He said his body was hanging to a tree in the cove. All the next day Ellen waited, but he didn't come. Then, when the full moon was up over the hill, Ellen ran screaming in the direction of the cove. They found her there by the body of Edward, who was hanging to the limb of a tree, hung by the rope that he'd taken to tie up the deer. Ellen had taken the end of the rope that was hanging down and had hung herself with it.

"Folks always said that the brothers had hung Edward, but they had no witnesses, and so it was judged to be suicide. It's a terrible tragic story, but there's a good lesson in it, for it shows what terrible wickedness there is in the world. If people could know a story like that, they might be turned against such wickedness.

"After that they say that at certain times, when the full moon just comes over the ridge yonder, the form of a woman in white can be seen running along the ridge toward the cove, screaming and wailing like a demon. I saw it once, and I heard the awful wailing, but I never looked toward the ridge after that when the moon was full. I don't hear so well now, but I do believe I heard it last night. Yes, I believe you two young people saw it and heard it. What could it be but the ghost of Ellen?"

THE LOVER'S GHOST

One summer evening in 1952, I went to the home of "Uncle" Louis O'Dell, in Nicholas County, to hear him sing some of the old songs which he said he used to sing for people over the telephone. When I asked him whether he knew any ghost stories, he said, "My wife can tell the stories better than I can." Mrs. O'Dell then told the story of the lover's ghost, which she said she knew to be true.

A handsome young man fell in love with a very pretty girl, and they were planning to be married as soon as the preacher came to hold meeting, which was about once a month. Just about two weeks before the preacher came, the girl got a fever and died. After the funeral, the young man asked the girl's brother to go home with him, for he said he couldn't stand to be alone. The brother said he had some work to do and couldn't go then, but he would come over some other time. The young man begged other members of the family to go with him, but each in turn put him off. Finally the young man went back home alone.

That evening two of the smaller sisters of the dead girl had to go out to fetch the cows in for milking. They had to pass the graveyard where their sister was buried. It was almost dusk when they came back past the graveyard, where they saw something white hovering over their sister's grave. They became frightened and ran home as fast as they could.

In a little while the father of the dead girl's lover came riding up on horseback and said that his son had hanged himself in the barn. The death of the boy was just about the same time that the girls saw something white hovering over their sister's grave. They buried the young man beside the girl he loved. They say that vines grew up from the two graves and twined their leaves together.

A HAUNTED HOUSE

This story was told by Oy Minney, of Gilmer County. He said very earnestly and seriously, "You may not believe it, but it is so, ever bit of it."

I was a-comin' home one night after dark and I saw a light in the kitchen. Well, I thought my wife was up yit. When I went in the house, no one was up, and my wife was in bed asleep.

One night I heard cats a-fightin', and I got up to put them out, but not a cat could be found. The hogs kept a-rootin' in the trough, and when I butchered them they kept right on a-rootin' so that I could hear them of a night.

One night I woke up and the house was full of smoke. I jumped up, opened the doors and windows, and started to wake the rest of the family up. Suddenly the smoke all left, and not a trace of fire could be found. I looked all over the house the next day, but couldn't find a sign of fire. Sometimes I could hear water gurglin' under the ground, and it would move from place to place. I never was able to locate it.

I saw a woman dressed in white, who came near the house several times but never came in the house. Several years after I moved out of this house, I was takin' care of a sick person at the next house below, and the third night I was there I saw the same woman dressed all in white.

There was a brown stain on the floor in the kitchen of the haunted house. We tried a good many times to remove the stain, but never could git it off.

When Uncle Joel Dobbins moved in there he heard strange things. One night it sounded like someone puttin' a backlog on the fire, but he couldn't find anything out of place. Uncle Joel asked the Lord to show him what the trouble was. One evening he was a-settin' by the fire, and a little girl about three years old laid her hand on his knee. When he took his eyes offen her and then looked back, she was gone.

One man said he heard a woman scream in that house one day as he was a-passin' there. My grandmother, who lived about a mile above the haunted house, said that smoke came from the house and covered Oke Stump as he rode by. She said she kept her windows closed at night to keep out the smoke that came from this house. She said it had come in two or three times when she forgot to close her windows.

The reason the house was haunted was that a man was supposed to have killed his wife and two children there. The story is that when he moved into this house he had a wife and two children with him, but when he left he was alone. No one ever found out what he did with them.

THE POLTERGEIST OF PETERSBURG

A poltergeist (literally a noise-ghost) is a spirit that makes its presence known by throwing objects about a room, making loud and unpleasant noises, and generally making life miserable for the people living in the house. It is not the spirit of a departed person, but probably a spirit in the service of the devil. Arnold Snyder, a student in my extension class at Petersburg, West Virginia, told the story of the poltergeist as he had heard it from several people who live there.

A ghost appeared in a house in Powers Hollow in the year of 1910, before a railroad was thought of in Petersburg. This spirit first appeared to two children who were sleeping upstairs in a room alone. It began to pull the cover and to ask them if they would like to have some money. They were afraid and said, "No." Later it appeared to the mother and father and told them to dig under a certain room of their house, and they would find money. It said that its name was John Power, and that it had buried the money during the Civil War, and wanted them to have it because they needed it. It also told them to read certain passages from the Bible.

Finally they dug under the house and came to an iron pot, which they presumed to be the pot of money. Before they opened it they began to argue over how they would spend the money, and right before their eyes the pot sank deeper into the ground.

The spirit would upset chairs, shake their beds, pull the covers off the beds, and cause dishes to fall from their hands. It would also tell them something of the future, such as when a railroad was coming to Petersburg, and when they were going to have callers. Finally the family moved away to get away from the spirit, but it would bother them wherever they moved. The mystery was never solved.

THE MOTHER-IN-LAW'S REVENGE

Mrs. John Harper, of Braxton County, West Virginia, was eighty-seven years old when she told this story, which had been told to her by her father, Dr. B. H. Adkinson. Dr. Adkinson was an "old-time" doctor who "studied medicine" under Dr. Evans, an Indian doctor who used roots and herbs.

My parents went to Pocahontas County shortly after they were married, and moved into a rather large house. Not far from the main building was a smaller house which they were told had been used by previous owners as a cooking house.

Father had gone out to look over the property, while mother went about the work of unpacking their belongings and washing the dishes. As she had not cleaned the cupboards, she placed the dishes on a large table in the dining room. All at once she heard a terrific noise as if the table had upset and all the dishes had crashed on the floor. She rushed into the dining room, but there was nothing wrong. When she returned to the kitchen, the terrible noise occurred again. She was terribly frightened, and when her husband returned she related the happenings to him. She told him she could not live there. Her husband tried to ease her fears, telling her that it was just that she was alone, and noises seemed greater than they really were. Just then it sounded again. This time her husband went to investigate, but he found nothing wrong. The noises continued through the night. Convinced that the house was haunted, they moved away from there as soon as they could find another house.

Later they learned about the reason for the noises in the haunted house. The family who had built the house did not get along very well together. The daughter-in-law was very mean to her husband's mother. Finally the husband was forced to build the smaller house for his mother, so that she might have a little comfort during the last years of her life on earth. The wife continued to be very mean to her mother-in-law in every way possible. After the old lady's death, she got even with her daughter-in-law by returning in spirit and making the noises that finally made it impossible for them to live in the house. However, the noises did not cease with their leaving, but continued to frighten anyone who occupied the house.

THE GHOST RIDER

Very rarely does a folk ballad become a folk tale, which survives in tradition as a prose tale. The original of this story of the ghost rider, told to me by Bud Workman, of Raleigh County, is undoubtedly the old ballad, "The Suffolk Miracle." I have found the ballad surviving also in this same region of the state, but I know of no other ballad that has become a prose tale.

Once there was couple that had a beautiful daughter, and they thought she was about the finest thing in the whole world. They took her to the city often and saw that she got to meet important people. They were sure that some day she would marry a rich man. This family was pretty well-to-do and had a big house in the country, with lots of people working on their estate, and they owned the finest riding horses.

There was a young man working for them who was a good horseman. He could ride any horse on the place. Well, they got this young man to teach their daughter to ride. They say she got so that she could ride just about as well as any man.

One day the girl came in home looking happy and laughing. And she said to her father, "Daddy, you know I like Jim." (The young man's name was Jim.) Well, they knew right away that the two young people had fallen in love. So the father and mother talked it over, and they decided that it would be a good thing to send the girl to the city to go to school and live with her uncle so that she would get over her feeling for this farmer boy. The girl didn't want to go, but finally she had to give in. The city where the uncle lived was three hundred miles away, and she was expected to stay there for at least a year.

When Jim heard about it he thought he couldn't stand it, for he loved her so much he said he'd rather die than live without her. When he told her goodby, he said he wished he had something to give her so that she would always think of him. "Just give me your handkerchief," she told him, "And I'll always carry it with me." He gave her his best handkerchief, and as she was leaving she waved to him with it.

Well, after she left he grieved so much that he took sick and had to go to bed. There was nothing they could do for him that would get him out of that bed. In about two weeks he died. The people all around said that he died of a broken heart.

The girl went to her uncle's house, but she wasn't very happy because she was still in love with Jim. Many times she used his handkerchief to hold her tears. A year passed and she never heard anything from him. Then one night there was a knock at the door, and when she went to the door, there stood Jim. He told her that her father had sent him to fetch her back home. She hurried up and got ready to go, and he took her on the horse behind him. They rode almost as fast as the wind, and she held on to him. After a while he said, "I've got an awful headache." "Here, let me tie this handkerchief around your head," she said. And she tied around his head the handkerchief that he'd given her. Then he turned around to her, and she kissed his lips. "My, Jim," she said, "Your lips are colder than the clay."

He never said a word, but rode on faster than ever, until before long they were back at the house of her parents. She got off and knocked on the door. When her father came to the door she put her arms around his neck and thanked him for sending her lover to fetch her back home. "Your lover!" the father exclaimed, "Why, that man has been dead for a year!"

They looked around, but her lover had disappeared. They found the horse standing near the grave where Jim was buried. The father went to the judge of the district and got permission to open the grave, and there they found Jim's corpse with the handkerchief tied around his head.

It wasn't long then till the girl took sick and died. They buried her in the graveyard beside Jim, just as she asked them to do before she died.

THE GHOST RIDES WITH HER LOVER

An elderly gentleman in Raleigh County, who asked me not to divulge his name, told me this story of his own experience.

I was just a young fellow when I started a-courtin' that girl who lived over the hill from our place. I had a good ridin' horse—he could out-run any horse I ever saw—and I'd go every Saturday evening on my horse to see that girl. I won't give you her name, because some of her folks still live over there, and I don't want them to know about what happened to me.

My family didn't want me to marry this girl. They didn't have anything agin her, but they said I was too young to get married, and I don't think they cared much for her family, mostly because they were Republicans, and my family has always been strong Democrats.

She said we could run away and get married without our folks knowin' about it, but I wouldn't do that. Well, we quarreled over it, and I didn't go over there for a while. Then one day her brother came to tell me his sister had taken a bad fever and was awful poorly. He said she was a-callin' for me, and would I come over.

I went at once, but when I got there she was dead. When they had the wake I'll never forget how that shepherd dog that she had, the one that hung around her so much, howled all night. It sounded just like a woman a-screamin', and they couldn't make it stop. The girl was buried in the graveyard up there by the road.

It was only a week later that I rode over to the village to get some things at the store on a Saturday evening. I got to talkin' to some people at the store and stayed later than I intended, so that it was after dark when I got started for home. The moon was out enough that I could see pretty well. I got just about a half mile the other side of that graveyard, when all of a sudden I felt something on behind me on my horse. It felt like a woman was a-ridin' behind me, and I could feel her arms around my waist so tight I had trouble a-breathin'. I spurred my horse, and I never saw my horse run so fast, but still that thing hung on to me. Then, just as we passed that graveyard, it seemed like all of a sudden there was nothing on behind me, and my horse calmed down.

I was sure it was the ghost of the girl who was buried there in that graveyard. After that I would never ride that road again after dark.

THE DOG GHOST OF PEACH TREE

Folk tales in which the ghost of a dog, or any other animal, appears in a visible form are very rare among the mountain people. "Uncle" Bud Workman, of Raleigh County, an excellent narrator, told the story of the dog that appeared in the neighborhood where he lived.

About the year 1880, at a place in Raleigh County called Peach Tree, a big brindle dog was seen by many of the residents of this place. It was a very large dog, but it never did any harm to anyone. But since nobody claimed it and people were afraid of it, they tried to kill it. One person threw rocks at it from a short distance, but he said the rocks went right through the dog. A preacher shot the dog five times from only five feet away, but the shots all passed right through it and didn't even bother it.

One night this dog came up the road and passed the house where there were the meanest dogs in the country, but when this dog came near the house, these mean dogs tucked their tails between their legs and ran back under the house.

The dog was seen for about three weeks, always at night and never in daylight. Lots of folks wouldn't go out at night for fear of meeting that dog. Finally it disappeared and was not seen any more.

THE HITCH-HIKER

The story of the hitch-hiking ghost has been told in many parts of America, always with a different setting. One version, set in 1934 in Chicago, tells of a taxi driver picking up a Catholic nun, who directed him to take her to her convent. On the way, she told him many things that would come to pass in the future, including the prophecy of a second world war to take place in a few years. When he arrived at the convent, he opened the taxi door to help his passenger out, and to his amazement she had disappeared. He went to the convent and told his story to the nun who came to the door. Looking up, he saw on the wall a picture of the nun who had been his passenger.

"Why, that is the one!" he exclaimed.

"Yes, that is Mother Cabrini," said the nun. "She died in 1917."

The following story of the hitch-hiking ghost was contributed by Doris Lilly, a student in my class in folklore at West Virginia University in 1955. She heard the story from the family of the girl who was killed.

Late one night a man was driving alone in his automobile on Highway 33, not far from Elkins, West Virginia. Just after he crossed a bridge, he saw a young woman standing at the side of the highway, waving her hand as a signal that she wished to be given a ride in the direction of Elkins. He opened the door for her, and she sat down in the seat beside him. She told him that her parents would be worried, for she was very late because of trouble she had with her car.

When he arrived at the address she had given him, he stopped and went around the car to open the door for her. She had disappeared. He knocked on the door of the house where she had said she lived, and a middle-age woman answered. He explained what had happened, and asked if the girl had come into the house.

"Oh, yes, I understand," the woman said. "That was my daughter's ghost. She was killed in an auto accident out there at that bridge on Highway 33, just two years ago. You are not the first one to bring her ghost here to her home."

THE PHANTOM WAGON

From several persons living in the vicinity of Flatwoods, a small village in Braxton County, West Virginia, I have heard the story of the phantom wagon. Since the various accounts differ in some details, I am re-telling the story to include all of the pertinent details.

On a country road in Braxton County a loaded wagon drawn by a four-horse team approaches a small hill where the horses have to pull hard to keep the wagon moving. All four horses are milk-white, equipped with black harness studded with shining brass. On the wagon seat holding the reins is a young man who appears to be in his thirties. Sitting close beside him is a young woman, dressed in a long white dress, with golden hair hanging to her waist. The wagon is loaded with the things which pioneers brought with them to start their mountain homes.

Slowly the wagon moves up the hill until the lead horses reach the crest of the incline, and suddenly there is nothing there. The horses, the wagon, and the couple, all have disappeared.

Several persons have seen this mysterious phenomenon. One elderly man said he was on that road one night when he was a young man. He was on his way home after calling on a girl. He said the moon was out and he could see pretty well without a light. He said he'd never forget that sight as long as he lived, even if he lived to be a hundred years old.

From several sources I have heard versions of the story accounting for the strange apparition. Some people might say it is nothing but an optical illusion, but all of the details of the scene as described by the grandfather of one of the narrators are too clear to be dismissed as an illusion. He said that long ago, when this road was nothing but a trail, a young couple had planned to settle not far from the spot where the "hant", as he called it, was seen. It was moonlight, and they decided to keep going after dark so that they could camp for the rest of the night on Hacker's Creek. Just as they reached the top of the little hill, a band of Indians attacked them and killed them. The Indians drove the horses and wagon away and left the dead couple lying by the side of the road. Since then, even now, when the moon is shining on certain nights, the young couple can be seen driving their wagon near the top of the hill until they disappear near the top.

ADD'S IMAGE

This story was told by James Floyd to his granddaughter, Mrs. Teddy Peters, of Glenville, who told it to me in 1952.

The setting of this story was the old Gluck house about three miles from Glenville. The old log house was later covered with weather-boarding. The time of the story was during the Civil War.

There were two boys and two girls in the family after the mother had died and the father had been made a prisoner of war. The oldest girl was taking care of the family during the war. One day a group of Confederate soldiers came along and took the youngest boy, Add, with them. Thomas R. Floyd, being the closest neighbor, took the rest of the children while the oldest sister went away to try to get her father released. Then she traveled many miles trying to find her brother, Add, but she never succeeded. The last time he had been seen he was with Side Campbell's regiment, sitting on a stump by himself eating roast corn. One evening, she was told, he was sent through the woods after water and never returned to the regiment.

In the meantime James Floyd and his sister brought the children home and stayed with them. One night they were all sitting in the front room and talking before going to bed. The oldest sister was talking about how she could not find her brother and that she felt she would never see him again. All at once, she cried out, "Look toward the window!" They all saw the brother's face and head, and saw it float through the room and disappear against the wall. He was never heard of after this, and the family believed he was killed.

THE GRAVEYARD GHOST

Virginia Straw, one of my students in folklore in an extension class at Sutton, said she had heard her grandmother tell a tale about Virginia's uncle seeing a ghost when he was young.

My uncle saw a ghost on Birch River. One morning before daylight as he was going along in a wagon, he passed an old graveyard. He saw a white figure that floated along the road beside him and then floated off toward the graveyard. The horses were hard to hold, and his dog cried and tried to get in the wagon. He declared it was true, and he would never go down there before daylight again. My grandmother said it was the ghost of a man they had known, who was buried there in that graveyard. He had been killed in an accident, but some people thought he might have been murdered.

THE PEDDLER'S GHOST OF MAYSVILLE

Mrs. Jo An Harman, a student in my class at Petersburg, West Virginia, gave me the story of a peddler's ghost, which she heard from David Clause of Maysville, West Virginia. It is believed to be authentic by many of the local people.

In the late 1800's a peddler was traveling through the small village of Maysville. Following the routine of other peddlers before him, he stopped at each of the homes scattered along the countryside. It was not unusual for the local families to offer a peddler a night's lodging. At dusk one evening the peddler made the last stop before moving to the next community. Neighbors assumed that he stayed overnight in the small farmhouse, for no one saw him leave. Curious neighbors watched for the peddler, but he had disappeared.

One of the local men had considered buying some of the clothes the peddler had shown him, but he had not made the purchase. He readily recognized these clothes when the owner of the small farmhouse wore them to the village store a few days after the disappearance of the peddler. The daughter of the farmer wore some of the peddler's cheap jewelry to school. The people of Maysville were convinced that the peddler had been murdered, but they had no definite proof.

Almost twenty-five years later, a young man was calling on a girl who lived near the farmhouse where the peddler had stayed. Near the gate he heard a strange sound which he described as the sound of blood gurgling in a man's throat. He flashed his light in the direction of the sound, and it suddenly ceased, but it was followed by the sound of a flock of crows flying away from the spot. Many times when he came to see the girl, he had the same experience.

About five years later in a field near the spot where the young man had heard the sounds, some men were plowing for the first time, and they hit a rock which sounded hollow. The men dug around the rock and finally unearthed a huge sandstone, a type of rock which was not common in the area. The men pulled the huge stone out of the ground and found that it had been cut in half. Beneath it was a powder-like substance in the shape of a human skeleton. The men were afraid and would not dig more, and they put the sandstone back in the hole and covered it with dirt.

Many people have heard the same noise there for the past seventy years, and no one has ever been able to explain it. Many people believe that it is the spot where the murdered peddler was buried.

THE GHOSTS OF ECHO ROCK

The very dear old lady in Raleigh County who told me the following story, said, "Now if you ever put this story in a book, don't put it in the book that I told it to you. It is a part of our family tradition, but there are some younger members of the family who might not like the way I tell it."

I was just a young girl when all this took place, but I remember it just as if it happened yesterday. I'm ninety-four now, and I've lived my life. I'm just a-waitin' for the Lord to call me, and when He calls, I'll be happy to meet my husband over yonder, where he's been for almost twenty years.

There was a big family of us, five boys and three girls. We lived in that big house that you passed on the right of the road just above here. Granny was a-livin' with us then. She was Pa's mother, and after her husband died, she made her home with us. I was the youngest of the family. Pa and Ma were both very religious people, and they taught us all to try to live to please the Almighty. All of us could sing right well, and we sang a lot in our home—mostly the old-time religious songs. Once a week we'd go to the church, where people would come in and we'd have singin'. Everybody liked to hear my sister Nancy sing by herself, and every time we had singin' at the church, they'd get her to sing. She was the oldest of us girls, just eighteen at the time, and she was a pretty girl.

I remember that night when we were singin' at the church, the first Wednesday night in June. We were singin' the old hymn, "The Ninety and Nine", when there was a sound at the door, and a young man walked in, trying not to make any noise. He was carrying a kind of pack on his back. He set the pack down just inside the door and took a seat in the back of the church. He listened to us almost like a person who was spellbound. When we finished the song, my Pa, who was the song leader, spoke to the young man, and told him we'd be proud to have him join us. He said he'd like to listen to us, for he said he'd never heard such beautiful singin' in his life.

Then some of the folks asked Nancy to sing, and when she stood up and sang, I never saw such a look of love in anybody's face as that young man showed.

I remember the song that Nancy sang, "All My Life Long." It was the song she liked to sing so well, and my, how she could sing it! When she finished the song, the young man came up and told who he was and how he came to be there. His name was Charles Parker, and he had come from New York City. He said he'd traveled all the way to Grafton, West Virginia, by train, then got off the train and started walking over the hills to the south. He said he had stopped at people's houses to eat, and stayed the nights with families who asked him to stay. A few nights he had slept in a hayloft when there was no room in the house. He was not a tramp, and he had plenty of money to pay his way. He said he had wanted to get away from the big city and hike through the hills where he could meet good people.

Pa and Ma both invited him to come home with us, for there was an extra bed in the cellar house where two of the boys slept, and he was welcome to stay up there with them.

When singin' was over we all walked back home—it was only a little piece to our house. He walked close to Nancy and talked to her most of the time, but she was still pretty bashful and didn't say much, but I could tell she was pleased to have his company.

When we got home, we sat out on the porch a while, and Charles told us about his family. His father was a wealthy store-man in New York. He wanted Charles to go into the store business with him, but Charles said he didn't like business. He went to college and studied music, and he wanted to be a singer. His father said that if that was what Charles wanted, he would help him. He had one of the best singin' teachers in all New York City, a man who used to be one of the big opera singers.

Charles said he worked hard for more than a year, getting ready to give a big public recital. They rented a big hall in the city, and they had a lot about it in the papers. Finally everything was ready for the big night in late May. There was a big crowd there, but Charles said it was most likely that most of them came because his father was well known. The people seemed to like the way he sang, and Charles said he thought he did all right. But the next day some of the papers had bad criticism about him. Most of them said that he had good tone, but there was something lacking in his singin'. One of the biggest critics said that Charles lacked the soul of a great singer.

Charles said it made him feel like he just had to go away somewhere, he didn't care much where it was. They talked it over at home, and they decided it might be a good thing for Charles if he took this kind of a trip. He said that now he felt like some strange force had led him to the little church where he heard us and got to meet us.

Well, all of us took a liking to Charles. He went out to the field and hoed corn along with the boys while Pa did the plowing. But we could see that Nancy had really fallen in love with him, and there was no doubting what he thought of her. In the evening they would walk down to that big rock yonder, that we always called "echo rock," because you stand a little piece from it and speak or sing, and the rock would throw the sound right back at you. Charles had a fine voice, and he made up a kind of little song that Nancy and he would sing to each other. They would sing a couple of words, then let it come back off the rock, then sing two more, till the other one would take up the song. Charles would sing:

Do you love me? And will you be mine for-ev - er?

Then Nancy would sing back to him:

I do love you, And I will be thine for-ev-er - more.

Of an evening we would all sit on the porch till time to go to bed. We would sing a lot, and Charles would tell us all about things in New York. He liked to hear Granny tell ghost tales and stories about the witches that Granny knew about. She was pretty old and was a little childish, but she could tell some good stories, and I'm sure she really believed in witches. Charles stayed with us for two weeks, when one evening when we were all on the porch he said he had something wonderful to tell us. He said he wanted to make Nancy his wife, and that she had given her consent. He said he knew it seemed to be rather sudden, but he felt that he'd been guided here to find Nancy. He said he'd never been so happy in his life, and he promised he'd make Nancy very happy. He said he would go back to his home in New York and make the arrangements with his parents, and then in about two weeks he'd come back, and they wanted to be married in the little church where he first saw her. Of course, we were all happy, because we all had taken a powerful liking to Charles.

Well, after Charles left, it was a different place there around the house. Nancy didn't say much, but after a week we could see her looking out toward that echo rock where they walked

so much. Then she took a fever and had to go to bed. She didn't
want to stay in bed, but Ma insisted that she must be well when
Charles got back.

It was on a Monday afternoon that she sat up in her bed and
said she felt so good she'd like to have her song-book so she
could sing a song. She sang the first verse of her song, "All my
Life Long," when the oldest boy saw a deer run across the yard,
and he ran in the house to get the rifle to shoot that deer. He
grabbed the gun and started out, but just when he got at the
door of the room where Nancy was sitting up in bed, that rifle
went off and the bullet went right through Nancy's head. She
fell back without even crying out.

We had no way to let Charles know what had happened, so
all we could do was just wait, hoping he would come before the
funeral. But we waited for two days, and then a grave was dug
down there close to echo rock, which had been the place where
they always sang together. It was a beautiful funeral that was
held there by the grave, and lots of folks came in, and they sang
Nancy's favorite song, "All My Life Long," the one she'd sung
just before she was killed.

It was just two days after the funeral, about dusk and all of us
sitting there on the porch, not saying a word. Suddenly we
heard Charles' voice coming from down near echo rock, singing, "Do you love me, and will you be mine forever?" He and
Nancy had it arranged that when he got back, she would come
and meet him there, and from then on they would always be
together. Well, we all went down together, Ma and Pa leading
us, and it was Pa that went out to take Charles by the hand and
tell him that Nancy was gone. Then Charles saw the grave, and
he threw himself on it and began to cry out and curse the Lord.
I can still see my Pa as he raised Charles to his feet and stood
there like a preacher saying the hundredth Psalm: "The Lord
reigneth; let the earth rejoice. Make a joyful noise unto the
Lord." Pa was always one to learn the Psalms by heart, and he
could recite well.

When Pa had finished, Charles stood there with his head

bowed, and then we all broke into song, singing Nancy's song, "All My Life Long." We all walked back to the house then and sat on the porch for a while, nobody hardly saying a word.

Charles stayed a few days and made arrangements for a pretty tombstone for Nancy's grave. There's a little white fence around it now, and it's kept up by the money that Charles provided for that purpose. Charles went back home to New York, but he never got married. When he died, one of his aunts sent us a piece that was written in the paper that told all about the funeral.

For a long time lots of folks said that at night they could hear a sound coming from echo rock, that sounded like two voices singin' together, but they couldn't quite make out the words that they sang. Yes, I've heard them, too, and I know what they are, and I can still hear the words they're singing, almost as clear as when I first heard Nancy and Charles sing them: "I do love you, and I will be thine forevermore."

THREE HEADLESS GHOSTS

The unusual and frightening experience of Granville O'Dell and his nephew was told by Mrs. Kerta Williamson, the daughter of Mr. O'Dell. Mr. O'Dell was a native of Hominy Falls, and was eighty-five years old when he died. He was an excellent singer of old ballads, and was also a good story teller. Mrs. Williamson said she had heard the story many times.

My father and his nephew were riding through the country when night came on, and they stopped at a farmhouse to ask for a night's lodging. They were told that there was no room in the house, but they were welcome to sleep in the barn if they wished. Thankful to have a place to sleep, they were soon asleep in the haymow. Mr. O'Dell said that in about two hours after he fell asleep, he felt something press on his stomach, his chest, and then his head. At first he thought he was having a bad dream, but when it was repeated twice he awoke. To his horror he saw three headless men walking over him. With a shout to his nephew, he ran from the barn, and they rode away from that place as fast as they could.

Upon later investigation, Mr. O'Dell was told that three men had been killed in the same barn several years before. This made him feel pretty sure that he had actually seen the ghosts of the three men whose heads had been cut off.

THE WHITE BIRD

Among folk stories there are numerous accounts of the passing soul appearing in a visible form immediately after the death of a person. The soul sometimes takes the form of a white bird, or it may be an indescribable white form that appears at a window. It is a beautiful thought that when a very old couple have reached the time when both must go soon, and one of them passes, the soul waits for its mate to go on the spiritual journey.

Mrs. Nancy Webb, of Raleigh County, whom I visited in the summer of 1958, told the touching story that happened to an old couple who were close friends of Mrs. Webb's parents.

Old Mr. and Mrs. Dick had lived a long, happy married life. When Mrs. Dick was ninety she passed on, leaving her husband of ninety-three, who grieved greatly over the loss of his wife. The neighbors went to help prepare Mrs. Dick for burial and to sit up with the body, as was the custom in those days. The night before the funeral, the neighbors were sitting and talking quietly, when they heard a noise at the window. There was a large white bird trying to enter the window. Three times the bird came and went, then finally disappeared.

Mr. Dick said it meant that he was to go very soon also. It was only a few days until Mr. Dick passed away to join his beloved wife.

THE GHOST
OF THE MURDERED STOREKEEPER

*On the Glenville-Weston road, about a mile and a half
east of Linn, there is a house now owned by Mr. A. A. Teter,
whose grand-daughter told the story.*

About the year 1910, a Mr. Stockard owned the farm
and dwelling. Directly across the road from the house was a
store which Mr. Stockard operated. One day while the family
was eating dinner, Mr. Stockard was in the store. They heard
a shot but did not go out to investigate. In a short time a cus-
tomer came to the house and told them that he had found Mr.
Stockard dead in the store. He had been killed with a shotgun.

The Stockard family moved away in a short time, and the
house stood vacant. Many people began to say that they were
sure the house was haunted. Later the house was bought by a
Mr. Holbert. He and his family did not live there long, for they
said they heard strange noises and they believed the house was
haunted.

In 1918, my grandfather Teter bought the farm and the old
store building, but he did not operate the store. At that time the
road was not hard-surfaced, and since traveling was slow, many
people stopped at the house to stay all night.

One salesman, who stopped at the house after my grandfather had bought it, said that after he had gone to sleep he awoke
suddenly to find the covers down at the foot of the bed. Thinking that perhaps he had kicked them off in his sleep, he replaced
them and went back to sleep. Later he awoke to find that the
same thing had happened. Again he replaced the covers and
went back to sleep. The third time he awoke, and this time he
saw a figure in white standing at the foot of the bed. It beckoned
to him to follow. He got up and followed the figure out of the
room, down the stairs, out of the house, and across the road.
Then the figure went behind the old store building, and he
followed. When the figure reached an old water well, it disap-

peared. The man returned to the house and obtained a light to search for the white figure. He could find only his tracks leading from the house to the old well.

THE GHOST OF THE MISTREATED HUSBAND

Madge Vannoy, a student in my class in folklore at Logan, West Virginia, in the summer of 1958, told this story which she had heard many times.

Old Mrs. Varner was a very cruel woman. She was so mean to her husband that she would make him go out in the field and work in all kinds of weather, even though he was sick at the time. One day Mr. Varner was very sick and didn't want to go out to the clearing to work, but his wife nagged him so much that he finally went out in the cold to work. All day he worked cutting brush and trees. Late in the afternoon she allowed him to come to the house, though he couldn't eat any dinner because he was sick. Late that night Mr. Varner died.

After that, strange cries and moans could be heard coming from this house. Some people who stayed there after Mr. Varner's death said that the house was haunted. They said they went to bed at night and locked the door of the room. In the night something kept pulling the cover down under the bed. When they pulled the cover back on the bed, something would give it a hard jerk and pull it back under the bed again. Then the door would fly open, even though it was still locked.

Once when a farmer and his son were passing the house, a huge dog walked between the horses and came out under the buggy. The horses didn't seem to take any notice of the dog. Many other people have seen a white figure walking about the place as they passed by.

THE PEDDLER'S GHOST
OF PENDLETON COUNTY

Riley Thompson, a student in my folklore class in exten-
sion at Petersburg, West Virginia, told the story of the peddler's
ghost of Pendelton County, which he had heard numerous
times.

In a two-story log house not far east of Riverton, West
Virginia, near the close of the last century, strange things occurred. A family by the name of Burn lived in the house. Every
night they would hear footsteps upstairs and the sound of a chain
being dragged over the floor. The disturbance was so great that
they finally had to move out of the house.

A peddler was supposed to have been killed in that house
many years before that time. There were blood stains behind one of the doors. They used everything they could
think of to remove the blood stains, but nothing would
remove them. Finally they removed the boards and replaced
them with new boards, but the stains came into the new
boards.

One night several people went to the house to hear the
sounds. When the sounds started, one of the bravest of those
present called out, "Come on down and show yourself." Just
then the footsteps headed for the stairs, came down and rattled
the doorknob of the door at the foot of the stairs. Nothing could
be seen at the door.

In recent years the old house burned down, and since then
no more stories have been told about the ghost of the peddler
at the old log house.

THE OLD HAUNTED HOUSE
OF NICHOLAS COUNTY

Mrs. Ocie White, of Nicholas County, told me the story of this old haunted house.

As long as I can remember, the old Jim Hanna house has been haunted. It is an old two-story log structure with a stone fireplace at each end. An outside stairway leads to the upstairs rooms. A row of swaying, whispering pine trees stands in front of the house, and the palings around the yard can scarcely be seen for huge masses of rambling rose vines. Large slabs of stone lead to the door.

Jim Hanna, an early settler of Nicholas County, built this house, cleared off a large tract of land for farming, and reared a large family here. He was known far and near for his bad disposition and violent temper. It was said that he beat his little girl almost to death. She died soon afterward, and everyone said it was from the beating. There was much talk among people living about there, and some of them were in favor of lynching him.

Not long after the little girl died, Jim Hanna sold his farm and moved to Missouri. From that time on, people who passed by the house at night told of hearing cries and groans. For several years my uncle lived in this house and slept in one of the upstairs bedrooms. One night he woke up and saw a girl dressed in a long white dress standing at the foot of the bed looking right straight at him. He said he pulled the covers up over his head, and when he looked again, she had disappeared. I have heard him tell this story many times. He is still living, and the old Hanna House is still standing.

A MYSTERIOUS DISAPPEARANCE

This story was contributed by Susanna Rose, of Braxton County.

There was a house just below my father's house in Braxton County that was haunted, so that no one could sleep upstairs. Several families had lived in this house, but no one ever put beds in the upstairs bedrooms.

An elderly man, who had built the house and lived in it, had brought a housekeeper to the house to do the housework after the death of his wife. She was seen around the place, but if anyone came near the house, she would go inside. Then one night she disappeared. Some of the neighbors saw the man hauling rocks in a sled and filling the well with the rocks. He then hired two men to dig another well on the other side of the house, telling them that an animal had fallen into his well and made it unfit for use.

After a few months, the man came home with another woman. She was seen around the yard, and it was evident that she was pregnant, but she never talked with the neighbors. Then one morning the man came to a neighbor's house and asked for someone to go to town to get a casket, for the woman and baby had died. He said he didn't know the time of birth was so near, and that his wife had gone into convulsions and died.

The neighbors helped bury the woman and her baby, and not long after that the old man died. The house was sold, and the new owner said it was haunted. He said that there were brown stains that looked like blood on the floor of one of the rooms. No matter how much they tried, they could not remove the stains, even though they used the strongest lye soap. Anyone who tried to sleep upstairs would be awakened by the sound of a baby crying, but there was no baby to be found.

After that the upstairs rooms were never used in this house. The mystery was never solved, but the brown stains on the floor of one of the rooms upstairs, the noises that made it impossible for anyone to sleep there, and the rock-filled well, all were there as plain evidence that there was an unlaid ghost about the place.

THE FIRESIDE GHOST

Mrs. Nancy Taylor, an elderly lady of Nicholas County, told the story of the little girl.

A family living in Nicholas County had a sick child. One night a neighbor girl was sitting in the child's bedroom attending the needs of the little invalid. Suddenly in the room there appeared the image of a little girl. The nurse followed her as she left the sick room and watched her disappear down the stairway.

When morning came, the nurse went home and told her story, insisting that her mother attend the sick child the following night. The mother did so. At the same hour as on the night before, the little girl appeared, passing from the room and down the stairway as on the previous night. The mother followed down the stairs and saw the child disappear just as she reached the fireplace. The other members of the family were told what had happened.

The father of the sick child called in the neighbors and asked them to search the house, especially the chimney corner where the little girl had disappeared. The men searched the whole house thoroughly, but they found nothing. At last someone suggested that the hearthstone be lifted. Underneath the stone they found the skeleton of a child. The bones were removed and buried in the graveyard, and after that the ghost was seen no more.

THE CHAIN

This was supposed to have happened in an old log house about one half mile above Orton. It was told by Edison Norman, whose mother, Mrs. Cal Norman, had told it to him.

The old log house had been built first, and some years later a lean-to kitchen was added. A small hall was built to connect the kitchen with the other part of the house. There was an outside entrance at one end of the hall, and at either end of the hall was a door, one leading to the kitchen and the other leading to the log house. A rolling sound, like the sound of chains being dragged, would come through the outside entrance, then go through the log house and up the stairs, turn and leave the house the same way it entered. It didn't occur every night, but only on certain nights about midnight. They searched for the cause of this strange sound, but could never solve the mystery.

THE HAUNTED HOUSE AT RENICK

This story was contributed by Margaret Ratliff, who had heard it from Wilma Sheets about her grandparents, whose name was Hardbarger. It took place in the small village of Renick, in Greenbrier County.

The house was first occupied by a Mr. and Mrs. Bryant. Mr. Bryant, who was track foreman on the C. and O. railroad, was called out one night to clear the tracks of a landslide. He and his crew worked late into the night and finally succeeded in clearing the tracks.

In the meantime, Mrs. Bryant, knowing that her husband would be tired and hungry when he returned, had prepared a hot meal for him. She was sitting in the kitchen reading, and she heard him come up the steps to the porch, walk over to a table on the porch, and set his lunch pail down. Thinking he would wash his hands and take off his muddy boots before coming in, she began to put the meal on the table. After a few minutes had elapsed and he had not come in, she walked to the door and called him. Upon receiving no answer, she went outside looking for him, but he was not to be found.

About an hour later a neighbor came and told her that on the return trip the motor car on which the men were riding had been wrecked, and her husband was killed.

A few years later, Mrs. Bryant went elsewhere to live, and the house was vacant until my grandparents moved there. The first night they occupied the house, after they had gone to bed, they heard someone sing the first line of the old hymn, "Rock of Ages."

The song ended suddenly with what sounded like a slap in the mouth. The next night when my uncle was returning home late, he saw a light in the front room, but there was no one there. On another occasion they heard steps outside, which then entered the house and ascended the steps to the second floor. Another time, when they entered the kitchen to turn out the light there, the light went out when they opened the door, although there was no explanation for it. During family prayer, all members of the family felt a cat rub against them, but there was no cat there. After living in this house for three years, they moved away. They said they couldn't get any rest because of all the strange things that went on there.

THE STROOP HOUSE GHOST

This story was told by Edward Fowler, of Logan County.

A family of five lived in what is now known as the Stroop house. There were the parents, two daughters, and one son. One of the daughters married a Mr. Preston Smith. The family was very much opposed to the marriage and did many things to antagonize Mr. Smith. Because of poor health, he was not able to work and had to live with the family. He finally became mentally disturbed, or at least the family said he was. His wife went to visit a neighbor one day, and when she returned she found him hanging in the woodshed.

There was no investigation, but many people did not believe that he had committed suicide. The wife went away immediately after the funeral, and the rest of the family moved to another state. They said they couldn't live in the house any longer because they heard moaning and groaning noises in the upstairs rooms.

Neighbors rented the garden for a few years, but everytime they went near the house they said they could hear someone moaning and groaning in the house. When they were on the porch, the noises sounded as if they were coming from upstairs. A group of young men went to the house to investigate. When they went in the house, they could hear the noises upstairs, but when they went upstairs, the noises seemed to be downstairs. The young men said that they could not explain the cause of the noises. Most of the people in the community would not go near the house, for they really believed it was haunted.

THE INFORMING REVENANT

This story was told by Mrs. Lenore Danley, of Glenville, Gilmer County, West Virginia.

Late one autumn evening, Preacher Hedges, a man whose word was never doubted, was standing at his gate near the ford at the mouth of Buffalo Creek, about two miles below Burnsville, on the Little Kanawha River. He heard a horseman coming rapidly down the road on the other side of the river. The horse splashed through the river at the ford, and as he came up to the gate, Preacher Hedges recognized the rider.

Preacher Hedges greeted him, "Good evening, Mr. Wright."

Wright answered, "This is not me, it is my ghost. I am lying in the river at my home at the boat landing. My family murdered me and threw me in the river. Right now they are pretending to search for me." Then Wright galloped up the road toward Burnsville.

Preacher Hedges quickly called some of his neighbors and joined the search. They found the body in the exact spot where Wright had told Preacher Hedges that the family had thrown him.

As Wright was a shiftless drunkard, and he had a well-liked and respected family of a wife, four daughters, and four sons, nothing was ever done about the murder.

A GHOST RETURNS FOR HIS HEAD

Venita Mullens, of Calvin, Nicholas County, West Virginia, who told this story, declared it to be the truth.

A bunch of lumbermen were working one day, when they had an explosion that destroyed several buildings and blew one man all to pieces. The other men gathered the parts of his body that could be found, but nowhere could they find his head. They buried him with a decent funeral. One night when the men were in their cabin talking, there was a knock on the door. One of the men went to the door, and there stood the man without any head, the man who had been killed. The man who went to the door was scared and quickly shut the door.

The men talked it over and decided it surely must be the ghost of the man who had been killed. The next night the same thing happened, and again they shut the door. On the third night, the ghost appeared again, and that time the man who went to the door asked it, "In the name of God, what do you want?"

The ghost answered, "You buried all of me but my head. It

is under that big rock over there by the oak tree."

The next day the men went to look for the head and found it where the ghost said it would be. They buried the head with the rest of the body, and after that the ghost never returned.

Ghosts can talk without heads, of course, for they are only spiritual beings.

THE WOMAN IN WHITE

This story was contributed by Mrs. Sylvia Cox, a student in the folklore class at Glenville State College. It was told to her by Venita Mullens, of Nicholas County.

The story had its beginning more than a half century ago at a house near Craigsville, known as the Cree place. A tragedy had occurred there, the details of which I could never find out, but it is said that a woman was killed there. For a long time after that when people passed there in the night, they would often see a woman dressed in white. She was always moving about the place. Some men said they were within a few yards of her and spoke to her. She never answered them, nor would she stop moving when she was spoken to. The mystery was never solved, but many people who saw the woman in white were sure that it was a ghost in the form of a woman.

THE HEADLESS RIDER OF SPRUCE LICK

This story was contributed by Mrs. Nellie McCoy Paugh, who heard it from Mrs. Dolly Stewart, of Sutton, Braxton County.

The story is based on an actual murder case. A good many years ago a murder was committed in the community now known as Spruce Lick. It is about six miles above Sutton on a branch of Wolf Creek, which is joined by a creek called Spruce Lick. Just a short distance below this junction of streams is the spot where the murder was committed.

A disagreement arose between two men because one of the men had been seeing the other man's wife. They met at this spot, and the enraged husband killed the other man and cut off his head. The head was thrown across the creek, and the body was burned in a brush pile.

Shortly after the murder, anyone riding or walking past this spot about midnight or early morning was likely to be accompanied by a headless rider. Sometimes he would grasp the bridle reins of the other's horse and try to turn it back. Most people who encountered this ghost would spur their horses and try to outdistance him. It was said that the horses detected the headless rider before their owners did, and the horses would try to run away from the ghost. One man rode his horse so hard in trying to get away that it took his horse a long time to recover. Many people still don't like to travel that road at night unless in groups of more than two people.

THE HEADLESS HORSEMAN
OF BRAXTON COUNTY

For the last hundred years people have talked about the headless horseman that appears in the low gap between the waters of Jim's Run of Clover Fork and Flesher Run. The story was told by Elizabeth Lee Kidd, of Braxton County.

Just at midnight this horseman can be seen riding his black horse down the hill at a gallop. The rider has no head. When the horse jumps into the road, the rider vanishes. The horse dives into the woods on the opposite side of the road and disappears. At the place where the horse disappears, a cow can be seen eating grass.

This horseman always comes out of the west along the old Peggy Falley line. The horse jumps into the road at the place where the line crosses the road.

The first person to see this ghost was an old black man who lived near the place before the Civil War. No one seems to know the reason why this mysterious ghost rider appears at this place.

THE GHOST OF SALLY ROBINSON

An old gentleman of Braxton County told this story to Elizabeth Lee Kidd, who gave it to me.

Now says I, I don't say this was a ghost and I don't say it wasn't. But this is just exactly what happened. I was a-comin' home one night about nine o'clock, and there was a pale moon a-shinin'. Just as I started out of the bottom field and up the bank, I seen a woman a-comin' down the hill. She had on a red and bluecheckered calico dress.

Now, I thought to myself, that is some one of the neighbor women that has been up to my house gabbing a while with my wife. For this reason I had no suspicion I was seein' something strange. Yes, I could hear her footsteps as she got closer. Just as I was about ready to speak to her, I looked up, and what do you think? She wasn't there. One minute this woman was within ten feet of me, plain as could be, and now there was no woman there. Where had she gone? I thought to myself: I think that was the ghost of old Aunt Sally Robinson, that the hogs et up many years ago right in the head of this holler.

There is no chance of seeing this ghost, or whatever you call it, except some nice soft spring evening or late fall. She never appears in winter or summer.

THE CRYING BABY

This story was also contributed by Elizabeth Lee Kidd, who has heard it many times.

It often happens that a strange thing may be seen near the Blake graveyard on Turkey Lick of Clover Fork. Just at dusk or a little later in the evening, if you are walking through the level bottom field, with everything as still as death, you suddenly hear a small baby crying. You look around to see where the sound is coming from. Then in front of you, perhaps about a hundred yards away you will see a white object rolling on the ground toward you. It appears to be a baby wrapped in a white blanket. If you run, the object will follow you. If you do not move, it will roll up to within ten feet of you and then disappear. The crying can be heard for a few seconds after the image has vanished.

THE GHOST OF THE CARD PLAYER

Mrs. Lenore Danley of Glenville told a number of stories which she had heard from various people when she was a girl. She was a student in the folklore class at Glenville State College. Her father told her this story.

Down on Rush Run two men sat playing cards one night. As the hour of midnight approached, one man had lost several hundred dollars in the game. He excused himself from the game, saying he wanted to get a drink of water. He walked around behind the other man, went into the other room and got his gun. He returned and shot the other man, whose name was King, through the back of the head. The murderer then took the body and buried it under the house. He was never punished for the crime, for since King's body was never found, it could not be proved that he had been murdered.

Later, a man named Greathouse moved into the house under which King's body was said to have been buried. There was a spot on the floor over which Mr. Greathouse would not place any table or bed, or any other object, for if he did, he said that at the same time of the night that King was supposed to have been murdered, any object that was placed over this certain spot, would be moved away by some invisible force.

AN ERRANT HUSBAND IS DISCIPLINED

Sometimes ghost stories are humorous, as is this one told by John Ward, of Chapmanville, Logan County.

There was a fellow who was awful bad to stay out late at night, sometimes till almost midnight. One night he told his wife that he was going down to get his boots repaired. She said, "All right, but don't stay out late."

When he was coming back home that night, late as usual, and it was very dark, he saw in front of him something standing there, white all over. Now, the man thought to himself that this was his neighbor trying to play a trick on him. He thought to himself, he would slip around behind him and scare him. He slipped up behind the figure and made a stab at it, and his arm just went right through it. He stepped back and thought he must not be close enough to hit it, so he moved up closer. He gave it another lick, and the same thing happened—there was nothing there to hit.

He got so scared, he grabbed his boots and took through the field a-runnin' as fast as he could, passed the schoolhouse and crossed over into the big road. He ran all the way home, which was more than a half mile. When he got just below the house, he cut around the back way so as to come in the kitchen. He was so scared he ran into the kitchen door and knocked it down. His wife was in bed asleep, and he almost scared her to death. He just fell over on the floor, and she had to help him up, he was scared so bad.

She asked him, "What in the world is the matter?"

"Oh," he said, "I didn't know that door was so easy to knock down."

Well, for a long time he didn't tell what had scared him so much. And it was a long time before he would go out at night by himself.

THE WALKING GHOST

This story was given to me by Dale Westfall, one of my students at Glenville State College in the summer of 1950. He said it was related to him by a friend whom we shall call John.

Several winters ago John's sister-in-law became very fond of a young man who was just starting his career as a teacher. He had taught but just a few months when he caught a bad cold. Because of the severity of the weather and of the great distance which he had to travel, his cold kept getting worse. At last his cold became so severe that he had to remain in bed and have an attending physician, but it was not long until the young man died.

The grave was prepared for the burial, which was to take place the next day. His girl friend, accompanied by her sister, went to the cemetery to inspect the new-made grave. As they were standing, looking silently into the open grave, they heard footsteps approaching from behind them. The night before, a snow had fallen, and it had frozen into a crusty, crunchy substance. The footsteps, as they approached from behind, made quite a loud noise, so that the sound was easily distinguishible to the two girls. When the girls turned around to see who else might be attending the burial place at this early hour, to their amazement, there was no one there. They looked for tracks, but none were to be found.

The girl, to this day, believes that it was the spirit of her lover.

THE GHOST
OF THE CRITES MOUNTAIN SCHOOLHOUSE

Anna Lee Cutlip one of my students in folklore in the extension class at Clay, West Virginia, told the following stories about the haunted schoolhouse on Crites Mountain.

Jess Clifton, who lives near the schoolhouse, said that he had always heard that the building was haunted, but he had never believed in ghosts, and therefore laughed about the tales he had heard about the place.

One evening as he was passing the schoolhouse, he heard a noise as if someone in the attic had dropped a large oil drum to the floor. He said that he stopped to listen, and it sounded as if the oil drum rolled all over the floor. After that he said he was sure the place was haunted.

Arnold Long, a native of Crites Mountain, said that one night as he was walking along the road which passes close by the school building, he saw a woman clothed in white appear in front of him. He stopped and watched as she came toward him and walked down a path into the woods. He said he was not afraid of anything until then, but after that he had a fear of this building.

One time when my husband was about fourteen years old he was visiting his sister, who lived about one mile beyond the schoolhouse. He did not leave his sister's home until it was almost dusk. As he came near the schoolhouse, he could hear voices singing inside the building. He went around to the side where he could climb up and look in a window. To his horror, there was no one in the building, but the voices were clearly singing. Even as he left the place, the voices continued the singing.

No one was able to tell me anything about why this place was haunted, and so, like much of our traditional lore, the story is lost.

THE HIDDEN TREASURE OF BEAR FORK

For many years a story of hidden treasure was well known around the region of Bear Fork, which empties into Steer Creek at Stumptown, in Gilmer County. The story was told to me by Gale Miller, a student in folklore at Glenville State College.

When Sam Lawson was about twelve years old he was compelled by a band of guerrilla soldiers during the Civil War, to carry a bag of money to a hiding place on Bear Fork. Before they got to the place where the money was hidden, Lawson was blindfolded until they had left the secret hiding place and traveled for a long distance. Lawson said it was a very heavy load he had to carry to the hiding place.

Many bands of persons have hunted for this treasure, but it has never been found. One day a man and his wife found a ledge on a cliff which they thought was the place where the treasure was buried. They put a ladder down to get on the ledge, when they heard voices. Not wanting others to know about their discovery, they hid the ladder and started toward the voices. After they had followed the voices for some distance, they heard them no more. The man and his wife went home, thinking they would return for the treasure, but the man died in a few days, and the woman could never find the place again.

Two other persons found a hole in a cliff and thought they had found the hiding place, but just when they were starting to investigate, they also heard voices. They left, but they could never find the spot again. Some say that the voices are the ghosts of the men who hid the treasure, and they are still guarding it.

WIZARD CLIP

One of the most remarkable combinations of history and folklore is the story of "Wizard Clip." We have put the story together from various oral accounts, from documentary sources, and from several visits to the scene at Middleway. There is no doubt that the story is based on real happenings that took place in the year 1797, for the case was investigated and reported by a capable and reliable investigator. But the story has been told and re-told through many generations, and thus has become a folk tale which belongs to oral tradition.

By the year 1797 Adam Livingston had established a home for himself and family on the banks of Opequon Creek at the edge of the village of Smithfield. The village was named for Mr. William Smith, who had obtained a grant of land there in 1729, and had established his home in 1732. Adam Livingston obtained his tract from Mr. Smith and brought his family to this beautiful spot from Pennsylvania. The name of the village was later changed to Middleway, which is located in Jefferson County, West Virginia.

It was a wild rainy night in 1797, as Livingston and his wife were sitting by their warm fire, that a knock was heard at the door.

"Who can that be on this kind of night?" asked Mrs. Livingston.

"It must be the wind rattling the door," Livingston answered.

Again came the loud knock, and this time Livingston opened the door. There stood a stranger, who said, "Good people, I would like a night's lodging. I am worn out out and can go no farther in this terrible storm."

"Why, of course you can stay," Livingston assured him.

In those days there were very few towns and few inns, and it was the rule to be hospitable to strangers. Livingston asked him if he had come far, but the stranger seemed too tired to talk. He was shown to a room and immediately lay down to rest. About midnight the Livingstons were awakened by a call from the stranger.

"I am sick," he groaned. "I am afraid I must be dying. For the love of God, get me a priest."

Livingston was a Lutheran, though his wife had been a Catholic. He had little sympathy for priests, and did not think it necessary now to go out in the storm to fetch a priest for a stranger.

"There is no priest nearer than Charles Town," said Livingston, "And even if I went there I might not be able to get one."

Along toward morning the stranger died without even telling his name. When day came, the neighbors were called in to help "lay out" the stranger, and to sit up with the body, as was the custom in those days, until the time of burial. Mrs. Livingston placed some lighted candles around the body, when suddenly a strange sound was heard, "clip, clip, clip," and one by one the candles went out. The wicks of the candles had been clipped off as if with shears. New candles were lighted, but the same thing happened. The sound continued, "clip, clip, clip," and little half-moon shaped holes were found in the clothes of those who heard the sounds. Word quickly spread around the community, and people who came heard the sound, and many had their clothes cut by the invisible shears.

After the burial, the strange happenings continued. Livingston had many misfortunes. His cattle died of murrain, and his crops failed. He lost a purse containing some money. But worst of all, he was plagued day and night by the incessant sound of the shears that went "clip, clip, clip." Even clothes that were locked away in the attic showed the little half-moon holes cut by the invisible shears. The bed linen, the clothing of the family and of the visitors who came there, even the saddles and harness, all were clipped. It was said that one woman came there wearing a cap. Before she entered the house she put the cap in her purse, for she said she was not going to have her cap ruined. But when she left the house she found that her cap, which had been in her purse all the time, was ruined by little crescent-shaped clips. Many terrible things happened, and Livingston was frantic.

One night he had a dream that he was trying to climb a mountain, but could not quite reach the summit, when a man wearing clerical garb reached down and took his hand, helping him up the mountain. Livingston thought that the dream meant that there was someone who could help him, and he immediately began searching for this man. One of his friends, Mr. William McSherry, told him to see the Episcopal minister, who had a church not far from there. But when Livingston saw this man, he said this was not the man in his dream. McSherry, who was Catholic, asked Livingston to go with him to Shepherdstown, where there was to be mass celebrated in a home, since there was no Catholic church there at the time. When Livingston saw the priest, Father Dennis Cahill, he exclaimed, "There is the man I saw in my dream! He is the one who can help me!" He told Father Cahill the story, and at first the priest suggested that perhaps the neighbors were playing tricks on him. However, Father Cahill came to the Livingston home, said prayers, and blessed the grave of the unknown stranger. Immediately things got better for Livingston, but the mysterious phenomena did not cease entirely until a requiem mass was said for the repose of the soul of the stranger.

In gratitude for his deliverance, Mr. Livingston made a deed to the Catholic church, effective on the death of Livingston, giving the church the tract of land of thirty-four acres on the banks of Opequon Creek, stipulating that a chapel be built there. Today a small wooden chapel stands there, and a field mass is celebrated there outside the chapel each year in the month of August. At the end of the field is a grave marked with a simple cross with the inscription, "The Unknown Stranger, 1797."

For some time the village was known as "Wizard Clip," but when the post office was established there, the name of the village became Middleway. Some people even yet call the land, which belongs to the Catholic church, "Priest's Field."

When these strange spiritual manifestations were being experienced in 1797, the Baltimore Diocese of the Catholic Church sent a young priest to Middleway to investigate. He was a Russian prince named Gallitzen, the first Catholic priest to receive all of his orders in America. He made a thorough investigation and wrote a report to his superiors. This priest became well known in the years after that and was called "The Apostle of the Alleghenies." He founded the town of Loretto, in Pennsylvania, and the town of Gallitzen, Pennsylvania, was named for him.

Folk Cures
❖❖❖❖❖❖❖❖❖❖❖

For people who lived in rural areas, a knowledge of first aid and the use of common medicines was important. It was often impossible to secure the services of a physician, and even today the situation is much the same. However, today's good roads have made it possible to drive to a hospital in a reasonably short time. But in earlier days, even for the birth of a baby, the mid-wife came to the home of the mother, and hospital births were almost unknown.

There were certain people who became knowledgeable in the use of herbs for medicines. These herb doctors were usually women, sometimes called "granny women." Their knowledge was handed down to them from other generations, and some of it had been learned from the Indians. Many of the folk cures make use of the common herbs and plants that grow in the fields and woods. A good number of the herbs used in folk medicine have been found to have real medicinal value and are used in well-known medicines which are sold in pharmacies today.

Many of the folk "cures" are nothing more than superstition. For example, the practice of rubbing a wart with a stick, then throwing the stick into a swamp where it will rot so that the wart will disappear, could not possibly be anything but superstition. However, numerous people have told me that they have had warts removed by this method. The passing of a baby under a raspberry bush to prevent whooping cough could be nothing but superstition.

Through the years I have recorded many of these folk cures, which I give here just as they were told to me. I make no distinction between those that may have some medicinal value and those which are obviously superstition. The reader may do his own research and draw his own conclusions.

ACONITE. This is a very powerful drug, used in fevers, pneumonia, erysipelas, and rheumatism. The tincture of the root is given in doses of one drop every hour until six doses have been taken. Care must be taken not to give it in excess.

ALOE. The juice of the plant is applied to burns and infections. It is said to be very effective. Aloe is often called the "Medicine Plant."

ASH. The sap of the ash tree is used as an antiseptic. It is applied to wounds to prevent infection and to induce healing.

ASAFETIDA. Pressed into cake form it was placed in a small cloth bag to keep away all kinds of diseases. Many school children used to wear it suspended from their necks. It is used medically to stimulate the intestinal and respiratory systems.

ASPARAGUS. This plant is sometimes used to promote the secretion of urine.

BALM OF GILEAD. Buds from the tree were boiled to make an effective salve for almost everything from backache to burns.

BEARBERRY. (Sometimes pronounced "Barberry.") A decoction is used in the treatment of chronic diseases of the bladder.

BASIL. The fragrance of the basil plant is inhaled to produce cheerfulness. It is supposed to be good for the heart.

BEECH. The leaves of the beech tree are applied to burns or blisters, or chewed for chapped lips or sore gums. The water found in hollow beech stumps is supposed to have curative powers. A tea made from the bark will cure weak back, and the tea mixed with lard is applied to cure rheumatism.

BEET. A wilted beet leaf makes an excellent poultice.

BIRCH. The birch tree has been widely used in folk medicine. The buds of the yellow birch are boiled to a syrup, and sulphur is added to make a salve for ringworm or for sores.

BLACKBERRY CORDIAL. It is used to cure "summer complaint."

BLACK CURRANT. The juice of the berries is used as an astringent in diarrhea for children.

BLACK HAW. A poultice made of the root of the black haw bush is excellent to draw a gathering.

BLACK OAK BARK. For diphtheria, boil black oak bark in water in order to get the juices from the bark, then add a sufficient amount of corn meal to make it suitable for a poultice, and apply the poultice to the throat of the patient.

BLOODROOT. A tincture of bloodroot is used as an expectorant, used in bronchitis and other infections of the lungs.

BONESET. A tea made of boneset will cure a common cold.

BUCKEYE. A decoction of buckeye bark is used as a nerve tonic and as a cure for fevers. The powdered leaves made into a snuff are good for catarrh and head colds.

BUCKTHORN. The bark is used as a cathartic, though it is likely to be very violent.

BURDOCK. Burdock leaves are used as a fever remedy. The leaves are bandaged point down to the patient's wrists and ankles. They are supposed to absorb the fever, which will run out at the points of the leaves. A string of burdock hung around a baby's neck will cure the colic. The roots are pounded, boiled, and made into a poultice for ringworms.

BUTTERFLY FLOWER. For kidney trouble, eat the root of the butterfly flower.

CAMOMILE. The flower, boiled and made into a tea, is a favorite folk remedy. It helps to expel aches, pains, and colds. It is supposed to be an excellent tonic, and is a remedy for pleurisy.

CAMPHOR. Camphor is a remedy that is found in almost all homes. It is used as a sedative for the nervous system in many disorders, especially the hysterical affections of women.

CARPENTER'S SQUARE. The plant makes a good poultice.

CARROT. The roots of the ordinary carrot can be made into a very good poultice.

CASTOR OIL. One of the most common purgatives is castor oil. It is sometimes used externally to remove warts.

CHERRY. All parts of the cherry tree have been used in folk medicine. A cold tea made from cherry tree bark is used to stop post-natal and menstrual hemorrhaging. The cherry roots are used to make a decoction which is used for syphilis. Cherry gum dissolved in wine is used for coughs and colds and is thought to be a good tonic. When a child has asthma, a lock of his hair placed in the trunk of a cherry tree is said to be a cure.

CHESTNUT. A tea made from the leaves of the chestnut tree is good for whooping cough.

CLAY MUD. Place clay mud on a bee sting.

COLTSFOOT. The dried leaves of coltsfoot are burnt and inhaled for lung infections. A poultice made of coltsfoot leaves is used to relieve toothache. Sometimes the leaves are used as a substitute for tobacco, which is said to be good for numerous ills.

COTTON ROOT. Used as a stimulant. A tea is made from the bark. It is also supposed to cause abortion.

COW MANURE. To cure a stone bruise, stand in a fresh pile of cow manure.

COWSLIP. The marsh marigold, or cowslip, sometimes called "palsey," is used for various remedies. The leaves are sometimes put in wounds. The roots are crushed, and the strained juice makes an excellent preparation for nosedrops. The odor of the flowers calms the heart and strengthens the brain. Wine made from the flowers, taken at bedtime, is a cure for insomnia. A mixture of the flower with linseed oil is used for burns.

OXEYE DAISY. Used as a cure for ulcers, for lunacy, and for wounds of the chest. A wine made from the flowers is used as a spring tonic. It is also used for the pain of rheumatism and gout. The juice of the leaves and roots is taken through the nose to cure migrain and to clear the head.

DANDELION. This plant has many uses. A tea made from the roots is used as a blood purifier and a spring tonic. It is also good for the liver and for rheumatism. Wine made from the flower is considered to be a good tonic. The juice of the stalks is used to remove warts.

DILL is used to relieve flatulence, colic, and obesity. The steam from the boiling of dill in water is supposed to stop toothache. Boiled in wine, the fumes are inhaled to stop hiccups. The ashes of the seeds are used in cases of scalding and for venereal disease.

DOGWOOD. The plant has many uses. The Indians used to make a tea of the dogwood bark, which they gave to their warriors who were fevered with battle wounds. It was used during the Civil War, especially by Confederate soldiers, for the treatment of malaria. It is supposed to stimulate the appetite. The raw berries were taken for the chills. In some places, an essence is made from the bark of the dogwood, and a few drops of it in a glass of whiskey is thought to be very healthful.

EGG. The white of an egg and salt mixed together makes a good poultice to draw a gathering.

ELDER. Thought to be capable of curing almost anything. A tea made from the bark is used for headache and as a diuretic. When the bark is scraped upward, it is supposed to be an emetic; when it is scraped downward, it is thought to be a laxative. Both the flower and the berry are used to make a tonic wine. A salve made of the flower and bark is used for the bite of the redbug and for the harvest tick. In some places, this salve is used for gout, burns, swellings, and tumors. The leaves are also used for poultices. The fruit is thought to be good for rheumatism, dropsy, and swollen limbs. The seeds are taken to reduce weight.

FENNEL. The seeds are used to relieve colic.

FERN. The large fern common to West Virginia is used in folk medicine. A tea made from the roots is considered a good cure for worms. A tea made from the leaves is a soothing application for burns and scalds.

FLAX. The seeds make an excellent poultice. In preparing the poultice, the seeds should be ground. When a foreign object gets in the eye, a flax seed is inserted under the eyelid to draw the object to it so that it can be removed.

FORGET-ME-NOT is used to cure the bites of snakes and mad dogs. The petals of the flower are used as a poultice for sore eyes. When boiled in milk and water, they are a remedy for summer complaint.

FOXGLOVE is used to stimulate a weak heart. It is also used as a flea repellent.

GARLIC is used for bronchitis and colds in the head. Made into a poultice, it is used for local inflammations.

GENTIAN is mixed in wine and used for aches and colds that have lodged in the joints. The root is sometimes used to stimulate the appetite and to aid digestion.

GERANIUM. A tea made from the root is used for infant diarrhea, for internal bleeding, and for kidney trouble.

GINGER. The root of wild ginger is used to cure sore mouth. It is also sometimes cooked with meat to prevent food poisoning.

GOLDEN ROD. An infusion, made by adding an ounce of the leaves and tops of the sweet golden rod to a pint of water, is used to relieve the pains of colic. A wine glass filled with this infusion is the ordinary dose.

GOLDEN SEAL. Commonly called "yellow root," it is good for sore throat or sore mouth although it has a bitter taste. To use it for sore throat, a tea is made by boiling the root in water, and it is used as a gargle. For sore mouth, the root is to be chewed.

HAWTHORN. Its flowers steeped in wine and distilled are good for all internal pains. The powdered berries in wine make a good tonic and a remedy for dropsy.

HENBANE. Used as a narcotic to quiet pains in inflammations. It must be administered with great caution, for it is poison.

HOP. The powdered root is used as a pill to quiet irritability of the urinary organs.

HOREHOUND. A tea made from the plant will cure a common cold.

HORSERADISH is used in the treatment of rheumatism, paralysis, dropsy, hoarseness, and is applied to the tooth for toothache. It is sometimes rubbed on the forehead for headache.

JACK-IN-THE-PULPIT. The bulb is given in very small doses for bronchitis, asthma, and rheumatism. Powdered and mixed with molasses, it is given to children as a cure for worms. The juice of the bulb is mixed with lard and used for ringworm.

JIMSON WEED. Used in a poultice for headache, rheumatism or other nagging pains. It is a very ill-smelling, poisonous weed.

JOE PYE WEED. Sometimes called "gravel root" because it is used as a remedy for gallstones and kidney stones. A tea made from the dried leaves is used to produce sweating. It is sometimes put in the bath of a fretful child to quiet it.

JOB'S TEARS. A necklace made of Job's tears is worn to cure sore throat, diphtheria, and goiter.

JUNIPER. An infusion made by boiling an ounce of the bruised berries in a pint of water is frequently used to stimulate the action of the kidneys.

LADYSLIPPER. To relieve nervousness, make a tea from ladyslipper roots and drink freely.

LARKSPUR. A tincture of larkspur is used for itch and asthma. It is a poison, and is sometimes used for its narcotic effect.

LAVENDER. Used to bathe the head for colds. The tea made from lavender is used as a stimulant tonic and for colic. It is also used as an antiseptic for wounds.

LETTUCE. Its leaves were used by the American Indians to brew a tea which they gave to women following childbirth to stimulate the flow of milk. It was sometimes given to babies as a sedative.

LILY. The roots of the lily are ground up and mixed with olive oil to be used for the hair. It is also applied to treat burns and poisonous bites, and for muscular pains.

LINDEN. The linden tree is very useful in folk medicine. Its flowers are made into a tea which is used for insomnia, headache, nerves, and to purify the blood. A tea made from the twigs is used for lung trouble. The inner bark is used to make a poultice for boils.

MARSH MALLOW. The root, boiled in milk, is good for cough medicine.

MAY APPLE. The root of the May apple is poisonous, but baking it makes it non-toxic. The fruit is edible. People in rural areas dig large quantities of the plant each year and sell it for medicinal purposes. A decoction of the baked root is used as a cathartic. The ground root is used as a poultice to draw the poison out of snake bites.

MEADOW SWEET. It is used to make an herb beer, which is used for curing colds and for stomach trouble.

MILKWEED. The milk of the milkweed is used to relieve itch and to remove warts. Milkweed and marigold boiled together make a good tea for menstrual pains. Milkweed tea is used to relieve gas pains and as a diuretic. The milk of the weed is put on cuts and scratches.

MISTLETOE. Long known as a cure-all, it is a remedy for epilepsy and hysteria. It aids in treating hypertension and nervous disorders.

MOUNTAIN LAUREL. The leaves of mountain laurel found in West Virginia are poisonous to animals, and the roots are very poisonous. A decoction of mountain laurel is used externally for the itch.

MUDWORT. Used in a decoction from the root fibers in a steam bath to give strength to old people. It is supposed to dispel weariness. A bit of the mudwort worn in a buttonhole is supposed to prevent weariness. The mudwort leaves steeped in hot water make a good eye wash.

MUSTARD. It has many medicinal uses. It is good for weak stomach, for clearing the blood, and for strengthening the heart. A decoction of mustard seed in wine is supposed to resist poisons, such as the bites of poisonous snakes. The seed taken in a drink is supposed to act as an aphrodisiac, and it helps the spleen and eases pain in the bowels. The seed is ground into powder and used as a snuff to cure head colds. It is also commonly used for a plaster to be used as a counter-irritant.

NETTLE. A tea made from the seeds or leaves of the nettle is used in cases of internal bleeding or nose bleed.

ONION. A fresh-cut onion will draw the poison from a snake bite.

PENNYROYAL. Pronounced "pennyrile," the tea is used for colds. It is also an excellent insect repellent.

PEONY. Used as an infusion for the relief of nervousness. The infusion is made by boiling an ounce of the powdered root in a pint of water. It is also used in epilepsy and St. Vitus' dance.

PEPPERMINT. As tea it is good for colic and as a tonic. The green leaves are to be chewed to relieve indigestion.

RED PEPPERS. Split lengthwise and moistened in vinegar, they are applied to the throat to cure quinsy.

PINE TREE ROSIN. It is applied to a cut or used as a poultice for a boil.

PLANTAIN. The bruised leaves make a good poultice.

POISON IVY. There are numerous cures for the poison from this vine. The following are some of the most common:

A. Apply gunpowder and sweet milk.

B. Ground-up burnt mussel shells.

C. Apply a paste of nightshade and sweet cream.

D. Apply lime water.

PUMPKIN SEEDS. They are largely used for expelling tape worms from the bowels. The patient should take no other food than pumpkin seeds and milk for a period of twenty-four hours, at the end of which time he should take a dose of castor oil.

RHUBARB. Used as a tonic. It is also used in cases of constipation.

ROSEMARY. An infusion of this plant is used as a tonic for the nervous system.

ST. JOHNSWORT. Used as a decoction to promote menstruation.

SAGE. An infusion of this plant is used to promote perspiration; it is given at the onset of fevers and inflamation.

SKULLCAP. Sometimes called "mad weed," because of its powerful sedative effect.

SLIPPERY ELM. To cure the "summer complaint," pour water

over the bruised bark of slippery elm and let it stand. Drink this water to cure the diarrhea.

SNAKEROOT. The wild plant called "snakeroot" in West Virginia is used in the treatment of colds. A tea made from the root boiled in water is supposed to break up a cold.

SAFFRON. A familiar garden flower which is used as a tea. For sore throat, boil an ounce of the leaves in a pint of water, and use it as a gargle. It is also used to break a fever. It is supposed to "bring out" the measles or scarlet fever.

STAVESACRE. An ointment made from the seeds of this plant is used to kill lice on the head.

TANSY. An infusion made from this plant is popularly supposed to be useful in bringing on the menstrual flow.

THORN APPLE. The dried leaves rolled into cigarettes and smoked are used to relieve asthma.

TOBACCO. The leaves are put on a wound to stop bleeding or to prevent infection.

WOOD SORREL. It was once considered to have value in treating cancer.

WORMWOOD. An infusion made by adding an ounce of the plant to a pint of boiling water is used for certain forms of dyspepsia. A full wineglass is the dose to be taken.

The following "cures" can easily be recognized as pure superstitions. Many of them are harmless, but some of them could be very harmful if used as a substitute for medical treatment.

To prevent the mumps from falling, tie a yarn string around the body under the arms.

If you take a knife and peel a piece of the bark of a peach tree downward, it will act as a purgative, but if you peel it upward, it will act as an emetic.

Wash your face in the dew before sunrise on the first day of May, and you will always have a good complexion.

To cure rheumatism, fill a quart jar with fish worms, set it out in the sun to render it out, and apply the oil.

The oil from a rattlesnake, used externally, will cure rheumatism.

Wear red flannel underwear, and you will not have rheumatism.

To avoid rheumatism, carry a buckeye in your pocket.

A man can quote to a woman, or a woman can quote to a man, the blood verse in the Bible (Ezekiel XVI, 6), and when this verse is repeated, the bleeding will cease. But if the telling is improperly done, the bleeding will not stop.

If you want a cut to heal quickly, keep the bandage tied with a woolen string.

If you cut yourself with a knife, stick the blade in the ground, and the bleeding will stop.

To stop a nosebleed, hold your nose over the sharp bit of an axe.

To stop nosebleed, tie a woolen string around your thumb.

To have good health, eat an onion a day.

To cure warts, wash your hands in stump water.

A ninth son can remove warts.

Drop the dirt from a newly-made grave on a wart, and the wart will disappear.

To cure warts, pick them with a pin and bury the pin.

To cure warts, take a hair from the tail of a gray horse and wind the hair around the warts.

To cure warts, steal a dishrag and rub it on the warts, then bury the dishrag. When it rots, the warts will disappear.

To cure warts, cut as many notches in a stick as there are warts, throw the stick in a swamp, and when it rots, the warts will disappear.

To cure warts, pick each wart until it bleeds, put a little of the blood from each wart on a grain of corn. Feed the corn to the chickens, and the warts will disappear.

To cure warts, rub a rock over the warts, wrap it up in a neat package and throw it away. Whoever finds the package will get the warts.

To stop a wound from bleeding, put spider webs in the cut.

Red flannel worn around the throat will prevent sore throat.

A posthumous child can cure the thrush (thrash) by putting his finger in the patient's mouth or by blowing his breath in the mouth of the patient.

Pass the baby under a raspberry bush, and it will never have thrash or whooping cough.

If you run a nail in your foot, grease the nail and carry it in your pocket, and the wound will heal quickly.

To cure the phtisic, bore a hole in a sugar tree the height of your head, and when the tree barks over, you will be well.

If there is a kernel (swollen gland) under your jaw, rub your index finger in pot black, draw a circle around the kernel, and it will disappear.

To cure the toe itch (athlete's foot), tie a woolen string greased with sheep's tallow around the crack.

If you get a pain in your side, lift up a flat rock, spit under it and replace it. The pain will then disappear.

Rattlesnake bones sewed up in a cloth bag and hung around a baby's neck, will help in cutting teeth.

Nature Lore
and Rules for Farming
❖❖❖❖❖❖❖❖❖❖❖❖❖❖❖❖❖❖❖❖❖❖❖

For one who depends on outdoor work for a living, it is very important to know what the weather will be for at least a day in advance. Today, with all the scientific and mechanical devices for predicting the course of nature, the farmer listens to the weather forecast on radio and television, or if he receives a daily newspaper, he may depend on the weather forecast which is printed there. However, before 1920, people living in the rural areas of the Appalachians had no radios, and comparatively few received daily newspapers. To know what kind of weather the next day or the next several days would bring, they had to depend on their knowledge of nature, which had been preserved in oral tradition for countless generations. If the farmer arose early in the morning to prepare for mowing that day and found no dew on the grass, he delayed his mowing, for he knew there would likely be rain that day. Or if the early fog rose quickly and hung around the hilltops, he was pretty sure that there would be rain.

People who lived close to the soil learned to interpret the language of nature. This knowledge was stored in the minds of people and handed down to future generations as a great treasury of unwritten knowledge, which is our folk heritage. Much of this heritage is forgotten and cast aside today, for we feel that there is no longer any need for traditional knowledge, when we can receive all we need to know from television, radio, and newspapers.

There were also numerous rules for carrying out the work on the farm and about the house. There were rules for planting, for harvesting crops, and for preparing them for preserving through the winter months. There were rules for the treatment of livestock and other domestic animals. In early days farmers kept in their minds a knowledge of the various signs of the zodiac, but in later years an almanac became an important item in every household. Many crops were to be planted according to the phases of the moon. Crops that developed underground had to be planted in the dark of the moon. If potatoes were planted in the light of the moon, they would have beautiful vines but small potatoes.

For half a century I have recorded this lore, which I have heard mostly from elderly people. Much of the weather lore is accurate and reliable for forecasting short-range changes in the weather. Most of the long-range forecasting is questionable, and no doubt much of it is pure superstition, just as are many of the planting rules, although I have known many people who follow them and have obtained good results. I am writing them as I heard them, without passing judgment on the accuracy or inaccuracy of any of them. Let the reader be his own judge, but I ask the reader to use caution.

Turkeys dance before a rain.

Sweating rocks are a sign of rain.

When the pitcher of water sweats excessively, it is going to rain.

When the salt melts, it will rain soon.

If the wool "snurls" up when you spin, it is a sign of rain.

When the insects fly low over the water, it is a sign of rain.

When the fish jump above the water, it is a sign of rain. (Note the relation of this forcast to the preceding one.)

If swallows fly low, it is a sign of rain.

If a lamp flickers continually, there will be rain.

When the corn twists, rain is coming.

A rain crow (dove) calling is a sign of coming rain.

When the tree frogs call more than usual, rain is coming.

When the fish worms come close to the top of the ground, it is a sign of coming rain.

If a rooster crows after six in the evening, his head will be wet before morning. (The midnight crowing of the roosters does not count in this forecast. The crowing of roosters at midnight, traditionally called "the first cock crow," is a natural phenomenon which I have never understood.)

If chickens pick their feathers after a rain, there will be a rain again soon. (This act of picking their feathers brings out the oil which prevents the water from soaking through the feathers.)

If the fog lifts early, there will be rain. (This is a result of low barometric pressure.)

Cows at peaceful rest in the evening indicate rain before morning.

If there is rain on Whitsunday, there will be rain for seven Sundays.

A ring around the moon with no stars inside the ring, means rain.

When gnats swarm, rain and warmer weather will follow.

When flies bite you, it will rain soon.

When the flies try to come in the house, it is a sign of rain.

When the red birds call in the morning, it will rain before night.

If the sun sets behind a cloud on Wednesday, it will rain before Sunday.

If it rains when the sun is shining, it will rain the next day at the same time.

When the evening's red and the morning's gray, It's the sign of a bonny, bonny day; When the evening's gray and morning's red, The ewe and the lamb will go wet to bed.

Rain before seven, clear before eleven.

If the leaves of the trees turn up on Monday, it will rain before Wednesday.

When the leaves of the poplar or grape turn up, it is a sure sign of rain.

When black snakes come out, it is a sign of coming rain.

There will be as many snows the following winter as there are rains in August.

If the smoke draws down the chimney, a change in weather is due.

When telephone wires ring, a change in weather may be expected.

If the camphor bottle is clear, the weather will be pretty.

The sun always shines at some time on Friday and Saturday.

A rainbow indicates that the rain is over.

The nearer the changes of the moon are to midnight, the fairer the weather will be until the next change of the moon.

When the Indian can hang his shot pouch on the corners of the moon, there will be fine weather.

When the smoke from the chimney rises straight in the air, the weather will be fair; when it spreads out over the roof, the weather will be foul.

When the fog lifts late, it will be a fine day.

When cobwebs can be seen on the ground in the morning, it will be a fine day. (The cobwebs can be seen when the dew is heavy.)

When the leaves of the aspen do not quiver, there is a hard storm approaching.

When the pigs run about with straws in their mouths, a storm is coming.

When the geese wander on the hills and fly homeward squawking, there will be a storm within twenty-four hours.

If the rooster continues to crow at short intervals in the daytime, there will be a hard rain within twelve hours.

When distant noises are heard plainly in the morning, there will be rain before night.

Lightning in the north is a sign of dry weather.

When the hornets build their nests high above the ground, it is a sign of a hard winter. If nests are low, it will be mild.

If there is thunder in February, there will be snow in May.

A late Easter brings a late spring; an early Easter, an early spring.

It always clears off in time to milk in the evening.

The wind always blows hardest at five o'clock, but always dies down just after sundown.

If March comes in like a lamb, it will go out like a lion; if it comes in like a lion, it will go out like a lamb.

If the groundhog sees his shadow on the second of February, there will be six more weeks of cold weather; if he does not see his shadow, winter is broken.

If the craw crabs throw up a mound around their holes, it will be a dry summer; if they do not throw up a mound around their holes, the summer will be a wet one.

When the locust blooms are heavy, it will be a cool summer.

When the shells on the nuts are thick, it means a hard winter.

When the fur on the animals is unusually heavy, it means a hard winter.

When the wooly worm is entirely black, it will be a hard winter; however, if one end of the worm is light, that part of the winter will be mild.

After you hear the first katydid, it will be six weeks until the first frost.

If the excrement within the bowels of a butchered hog is thin, the winter will be mild; if thick, the winter will be cold.

When the squirrels put away many nuts, the winter will be severe.

Thunder in winter is a sign of colder weather.

As deep as the ground dries out in the summer, so will the freezing be the next winter.

Thin corn husks mean a light winter; thick ones a heavy winter.

A cold winter follows a hot summer.

If the birds nest low, the river rises will be low that summer; if high, the rises will be high.

Thunder will cause milk to sour.

If your hair curls, expect rain.

Plant beets when the sign is in the heart.

To have good beets, let a growing person sow the seeds.

If you want tobacco to cure well, cut it in the new of the moon.

Plant cabbage and tomatoes in alternate hills, and the tomatoes will never blight.

To hoe beans, tomatoes, or potatoes when the dew is on will cause them to blight.

Plant cabbage seeds while the sign is in the head.

Sow early cabbage seeds on St. Patrick's Day.

Plant late cucumbers when the sign is in the twins.

Plant potatoes on Good Friday.

Sow flax seed on Good Friday.

What grows above the ground should be planted in the new of the moon; below, in the old of the moon.

Plant corn when the sign is in the scale, and the ears will be heavy.

Plant corn when the white-oak leaves are the size of squirrel's ears.

Plant corn when the dogwood is in full bloom.

Kill the first snake that you see in the spring, and no snake will bite you.

Always put wooden shingles on a house in the dark of the moon, or the shingles will turn up.

To keep a dog home, pull three hairs from the tip of his tail and put them under the doorstep.

Make all pickle stuff in the light of the moon, and the brine will rise quickly to cover it.

To make soap, stir it with a sassafras stick in the old of the moon.

Kraut or pickle beans will not keep if made by a woman during her menstrual period.

Beans planted in the new of the moon will climb up the corn, but if planted in the old of the moon, they will not climb.

Plant corn in the dark of the moon so the ears will be low and heavy.

A heavy dogwood bloom means a good corn crop.

Plant potatoes with the cut-side down for a good crop.

When the lilac bloom is heavy, there will be a good corn crop.

To ripen cider, set the barrel in the sun and place a black bottle in the bunghole.

Briers should be cut in August when the sign is in the heart.

To cut brush so that it will not grow again, cut it on Ember Days.

The new of the moon is the time to kill trees by ringing them.

Never peel the bark of a tree in the old of the moon.

Fruit is never killed by frost in the light of the moon.

There will be no fruit when apple blossoms do not fall under the tree.

Pick apples in the dark of the moon, and the bruised places will dry up; in the light of the moon, and they will rot.

Cut a limb off an apple tree in the light of the moon, and the stub will bark over; in the dark of the moon, and it will rot.

When you plant peach seeds, name them after women who have borne many children, and the trees will be fruitful.

If hawks get the chickens, pick up a flat rock from the creek bed, place it in the bottom of the grate, and the hawks will leave.

To break a setting hen, tie a red ribbon around her neck, with the bow across her breast.

Keep a goat in the barn, and there will be no sick animals there.

No matter what time of the day you kill a snake, its tail will wiggle until sunset.

Blacksnakes will suck cows.

Kill a snake that has sucked a cow, and the cow will go dry.

When a turtle bites, it will hold on until sunset.

A horsehair put in water will turn into a snake.

A toad will give you warts if you handle it.

If you plant climbing beans when the corner of the moon is

down, the beans will crawl on the ground instead of climbing the pole.

It is good to set an odd number of eggs.

Put your hand in the nest of a turkey, and it will not lay more eggs there.

Thunder kills chickens just about to hatch.

Butter will come easily all the year when you do not mix the milk of April with the milk of May.

When you move a cat, grease its feet so that it will not go back.

When you move a cat, carry it backwards, and it will not return.

The time to alter animals is when the sign is between the knee and the ankle.

When a calf is weaned in the light of the moon, the cow will not bawl.

If you kill a toad, the cows will give bloody milk.

If you milk a cow on the ground, she will go dry.

Pork killed in the old of the moon will shrink in the skillet.

Pork killed in the light of the moon will turn to grease.

Singe the hair of a rat and turn it loose, and all the other rats will follow it.

If you count your bee gums, all your bees will die.

When bees swarm, ring a bell or pound on tin pans to cause them to settle.

Hold your breath, and bees cannot sting you.

If a horse balks at night, he sees a ghost.

If you see a white horse, the next woman you see will have red hair.

A horse with big ears has a good disposition.

A white mule will never die.

When a foal is dropped, measure the distance from the hoof to the shoulder point. Twice this distance will be the height of the horse when it is grown.

Cut a fish worm into pieces, and each piece will make a new worm.

When two people hit their hoes together when working, they will be working together the next year.

When lightning strikes twice in the same place, there is mineral in the ground.

Sow grass seed in the light of the moon.

Sow wheat in the old of the moon so that the ground will sponge it up.

Plant flowers when the sign is in the sign of the flowers.

Set out onions in the old of the moon, and they will grow down; in the light of the moon, and they will grow out of the ground.

Plant radishes in the old of the moon.

Peppers will grow better when planted by a red-headed woman.

Sow turnips between sundown and dark, and you will never fail of a crop.

When there is much honeydew, the bees will not winter well.

Where greenbriers grow, the land is too poor to sprout black-eyed peas.

Look under white walnuts for ginseng.

The number of rows on an ear of corn is always even.

Frost will never kill peaches that bloom in the dark of the moon.

Superstitions

❖❖❖❖❖❖❖❖❖❖❖❖

It is almost impossible to trace the origins of many superstitions, even though they are fairly common to the whole world. The human being seeks the cause for everything that happens, and when the cause is not easily discernible, especially if the happening is something out of the ordinary or something that affects the course of human life, the mind tends to conclude that the cause was some prior happening or incident. For example, if a black cat crosses one's path, and very soon after that the person has an accident, it was the black cat that caused the bad luck. The human sees a relationship between the two events that does not really exist. If one puts his left shoe on first in the morning and has bad luck that day, the person concludes that if he had put his right shoe on first he would have had good luck. And thus a superstition originates.

Some superstitions no doubt have their origin in the efforts of parents to discipline children. For example, if you leave food on your plate, bad luck will follow. If you eat the point of your pie last, you will get your wish. Many children will leave the crust of their pie uneaten, but will eat it to have a wish fulfilled. It is bad luck to kill a hop toad. Toads are beneficial, for they eat harmful insects.

Perhaps it would be better if the superstitions that have survived in our traditions could be forgotten. Most of them are the

121

result of ignorance. It is an astonishing fact that most people in the world, regardless of environment, race, religion, or education, are superstitious to some degree. Education helps to destroy superstition, for superstition is born of ignorance and lack of reason.

Many superstitions are harmful, for they cause foolish fears that may do harm to the minds of people who believe them. The fluttering of a bird at the window of a home could arouse fear in the mind of one who believes it to be an omen of death. In my early childhood I heard from an old lady that when the lily in the corner of our yard grew up in four stalks in the spring, instead of the usual three, there was sure to be a death in our family. I looked forward to each spring with great fear that the lily might grow up in four stalks. I even dug off the top soil hoping that if I found four stalks starting to grow, I might cut one of them off and thus prevent a death. It is wrong to burden the mind of a child with such foolish fears, when the child's mind should be filled with happy experiences.

The superstitions that follow are offered as mere curiosities, with the hope that no reader will take them seriously. They are merely examples of odd beliefs that became a part of oral tradition. They do not reflect the character of the people of any particular region, except that some of them reflect the environmental influences which are found in the mountains and in rural living.

They should be entertaining, but they must never serve as guides for living. The student of folklore should find it interesting to attempt to trace the origins of some of these superstitions. For example, why is it considered unlucky for a black cat to cross your path? What is the significance of the black cat in folk beliefs? Why does a witch sometimes take the form of a black cat?

Why is it unlucky to leave a house by a door other than the one through you entered? How did such a silly belief originate?

Why is it bad luck to spill salt, but the bad luck may be avoided if you throw some salt over your left shoulder?

It is bad luck to kill a cricket.

If someone gives you flowers for planting and you thank them for the flowers, the flowers will die.

You should always leave a house by the same door you enter, or you will have bad luck.

If a picture is tilting on the wall, it means bad luck.

It will bring good luck if on New Year's Day you cook cabbage and black-eyed peas together and put a dime in them.

If the birds get the combings from your hair, they will make a nest of it, and you will always have a headache.

If on New Year's Day a male enters your house first, it means good luck; if a female enters first, it means bad luck.

If you are touched by a broom while some one is sweeping, it means bad luck.

If you sweep a circle around a boy or girl, he or she will never marry.

If you drop a spoon, a female guest is coming.

If you drop a fork, a male guest is coming.

If you wear a penny in your shoe, it will bring good luck.

It is good luck to find a penny.

It is good luck to find a button, if you keep it.

If it rains on your wedding day, it is a sign that you will shed many tears during your married life.

When you are moving, it is bad luck to move parsley roots.

It is bad luck to accept parsley roots from anyone.

It is bad luck to find an open safety pin.

To have good luck, always get out of bed on the right side.

Put your right shoe on first to have good luck.

It is bad luck to bring a hoe in the house.

If you kill a toad, your cow will give bloody milk.

It is bad luck to raise an umbrella in the house.

If you spill salt, you must throw some salt over your left shoulder to avoid bad luck.

It is bad luck to rock a rocking chair with no one in it.

A howling dog means death.

If four stocks of a lily come up to bloom, someone in the family will die that year.

If a person cuts out a window of his house and makes a door, someone in the family will die that year.

If anyone eats fruit that has grown in a graveyard, he will die before the year is out.

It is bad luck to step on the cracks in a boardwalk.

If a woman cuts out a dress for herself on Friday and does not finish it on the same day, she will die before the year is out.

It is bad luck to carry an axe in the house.

The dead must always be buried to face the rising sun.

A storm follows the death of old people. Nature is mourning.

If the walls creak, it means a death soon.

It is bad luck to watch some one out of sight.

If the thread knots while one is sewing, it means the one who is sewing will die.

It is bad luck to tell some one good-by.

It is bad luck to find a five-leaf clover.

It is good luck to find a four-leaf clover.

It is bad luck for three persons to use the same match to light their cigarettes.

Three lighted lamps on one table means bad luck is coming.

If you drop a dish rag, someone who is hungry is coming.

When the hands on the clock are straight up and down, put a cake in the oven and it will always come out well.

If someone jumps over you, your growth will stop.

If you eat pie on Tuesday, you will become ill.

If you eat fish and drink milk at the same time, you will be poisoned.

If you step over a broom, you will never be married.

If a bird flies in the window, someone in the family will die.

If a picture is broken in the home, the one in the picture will die.

If you receive a knife as a gift, you must give the donor a penny to prevent a broken friendship.

If your right hand itches, you will receive money.

If your left hand itches, you will shake hands with a stranger.

If you break a mirror, you will have bad luck for seven years.

If a baby looks into a mirror before it is a year old, it will not live to maturity.

It is bad luck to sweep the floor after the sun goes down.

It is bad luck for a black cat to cross the path in front of you.

It is bad luck to pass people on stairways.

It is bad luck for a hen to crow.

It is bad luck for a girl to whistle.

If a child's fingernails are cut before it is a year old, it will be a thief.

If you sing before breakfast, you will cry before supper.

It is bad luck to sell a hive of bees.

The hooting of an owl close to the house means bad luck.

Playing with a comb will cause a child to stammer.

When two persons are walking, it is a sign that they will quarrel if they walk on different sides of a tree or other object. The bad luck can be averted if they say, "Bread and butter."

When you buy a horse, it is good luck to change his name.

If you cannot find a lost article, spit in the palm of your hand; while saying, "Spitter, spitter, spider, tell me where that (name of the article) is and I'll give you a drink of cider," hit the spittle with your right forefinger. Follow the direction where most of the spittle goes, and you will find the article.

If you look at the moon through a knothole, you will never be married.

If two forks are at a place-setting on a table, the one who sits there will get married.

If there is a feather crown in your pillow it is a sign that you are going to heaven when you die.

When you pull a tooth, drive it in an apple tree, and good luck will follow.

Lightning-struck wood burned in the cooking stove will cause the house to be struck by lightning.

If you carry a rabbit's foot in your pocket, you will have good luck.

If you breathe on a bird's egg, the ants will eat it.

Hide a tooth under a rock and go back later, and you will find money.

If you take the last piece of anything, you will be an old maid unless you kiss the cook.

If a corpse is very cold, there will not be another death in the house for that year.

The man of the house must set out the rambler rose if it is to live.

When you find a hair pin, press it together. If the ends are even you will meet a boy; if uneven, you will meet a girl.

If you eat from an uneven plate, you will have bad luck.

If you shorten a baby's dress in May, you are shortening its days.

It is good luck to take a dog with you when you move, but bad luck to take a cat.

When a horseshoe is hung with the open end up, your luck will not run out.

A rabbit crossing your path will bring good luck.

To meet a cross-eyed person is a sign of good luck.

To lay your hand on the hump of a hunchback person is the best of luck.

This rhyme should be kept in mind while out walking:

> See a pin and pick it up,
> And all the day you'll have good luck;
> See a pin and let it lie,
> Bad luck to you will fly.

It is a sign of good luck to open the Bible at random and find the words "verily, verily" on the page.

When you get a small hen's egg, throw it over the house to avoid bad luck.

When you find a five-leaf clover you can give the bad luck away by giving it to another person, and he will have good luck.

To count the teeth in a comb brings bad luck.

It is bad luck to drop a comb, but put your foot on the comb that has been dropped and your luck will turn.

When you return to the house for something that has been forgotten, sit down in a chair before leaving again to avoid bad luck.

When you shake hands two times in saying goodby, do it again to avoid bad luck.

Thirteen people at the table brings bad luck.

Passing under a ladder brings bad luck.

Looking at the new moon through trees brings bad luck.

When playing cards it is bad luck to pick up the cards one at a time as they are being dealt.

It brings bad luck to play cards across the grain of the table.

It is bad luck to sit in a rocking chair to play cards.

For a lamp chimney to break in the hand without apparent cause is a sign of bad luck.

It is bad luck to change a baby's name.

It is bad luck to close an open gate.

To turn a coffin in the house will bring bad luck.

It is bad luck to postpone a wedding.

It is bad luck to carry a fishing pole into the house.

When hunting, it is bad luck to cross a different part of the fence from the person in front of you.

It is unlucky to throw a gift away.

To break something on New Year's day will bring bad luck for the rest of the year.

It is unlucky to marry a person born in the same month.

It is bad luck to spill ink.

To wash the palm of a baby's hand will wash his luck away.

It is bad luck for two persons to make a bed.

It is bad luck to burn bread.

It is bad luck to count the box cars in a train.

It is bad luck to count the carriages in a funeral procession.

If sassafras is burned in the fireplace, bad luck will follow.

To shake the table cloth after sundown brings bad luck.

To climb out a window and not climb back will bring bad luck.

If you sneeze while putting on your shoes, you must go back to bed to avoid bad luck.

To lean a broom against the bed will bring bad luck.

To sit with crossed feet in a rocking chair will bring bad luck.

To dream of gathering eggs is a sign of bad luck.

To move into a house before the fire which has been made by the former dwellers burns out, brings bad luck.

You can turn aside the bad luck when a black cat crosses your path by spitting on its tracks.

It is bad luck for a piece of bread to fall with the buttered side up.

If a clock stops without being run down, a dear friend will die at the hour at which the clock stopped.

If you hear three knocks at the door, someone in your family will die.

A falling star is a sign of death.

If a bat flies into the room, it is a sign of death.

When a cedar tree that has been set out has limbs long enough to cover the coffin of the person who set it out, he will die.

After a funeral, whichever sex leaves the graveyard first will be the next to be buried there.

If a filled grave sinks quickly, there will be another death in the family soon.

Hang your hat on a doorknob, and you are making the sign of a death in the family.

If a board warps in the porch, it is a sign of death in the family.

If a peach tree blooms twice in the year, it is a sign of death in the family.

If an apple tree with blossom on it falls, it means a death.

It is bad luck to lend money in a card game.

To change bad luck while playing cards, put on your hat.

To change bad luck while playing cards, exchange seats with another player.

To sit in a card game with a cross-eyed man will bring bad luck.

It is bad luck to start a journey on Friday.

Friday is an unlucky day to start anything you cannot complete.

To polish your shoes on your feet brings bad luck.

When you stumble over an object, go back and walk over it without stumbling to avoid bad luck.

It is bad luck for a whip-poor-will to light on the roof of a house.

To kill a spider brings bad luck.

For a picture to drop out of the frame means bad luck.

It is bad luck to cut the fingernails on Thursday.

It is bad luck for an animal to die in one's hand.

It is bad luck to boast of immunity from sickness, but the bad luck can be avoided by knocking on wood.

It is bad luck to count the buttons on another's clothes.

It is bad luck to visit a graveyard after dark.

It is bad luck to take anything from a graveyard.

It is bad luck to step or walk over a grave.

It is bad luck to meet a hearse.

It is bad luck for the head of the family to drown a cat.

To mend a garment you are wearing brings bad luck.

It is bad luck to change a garment that you have put on wrong side out.

A winding sheet, made when the melted wax clings around the candle and hardens, is sign of death in the family.

If a woman tears her wedding shoes she will be beaten by her husband.

If a pillow falls off the wedding bed, the one who lies on it first will die first.

Whoever sleeps first on the wedding night will die first.

As long as you keep some of the bread of your first wedded meal, you will never be in want.

If a bride breaks her wedding ring, she will be a widow soon.

If a wedding ring be lost, the couple will separate.

To awaken the bride on her wedding morning is bad luck. Let her sleep as long as she will.

For a bride to put her bare feet on the floor on the night of the wedding is unlucky.

If a bride puts on her left shoe first, her married life will be unhappy.

If you go into a vacant house, throw a ball of yarn and say, "I pull, who winds?". The one you are to marry will answer you.

Put the letters of the alphabet in a pan of water under your bed. The next morning the letter of your future husband will be turned over.

When two people meet on the stairsteps, it is a sign of a wedding.

Walk backwards nine steps, and you will see a hair the color of the person's hair you are to marry.

If anyone should see the bride's veil before the wedding, her married life will be unhappy.

If the bridesmaid is older than the bride, she should wear something green, or else she may never marry.

If a kettle of hot water is poured over the doorstep which the bride crosses, there will be another wedding in that house within the year.

For good luck the bride must wear:

Something old, something new,

Something borrowed, something blue,

And a gold dollar in her shoe.

Two lovers will never agree after their marriage if both wipe their faces on the same towel.

He who is needy when married, will be rich when buried.

If a boy and a girl meet by chance at a stile, they will be lovers.

Put three holly leaves under your pillow at night and name each leaf. The one that is turned over in the morning will be your husband.

Put a four-leaf clover in the Bible. The man you meet while you are carrying it will be your husband.

Hold the bride's dress on your lap for ten minutes, and you will be a bride within the year.

On the first day of May before sunrise, if you see a snail within a shell, your future husband will have a house. If the snail is outside the shell, he will have none. Sprinkle meal in front of the snail and it will form the initial of the man you are to marry.

Kiss a baby on the ninth day after its birth, and the next man you kiss will be your future husband.

Go fishing on the first day of May. A bite means a beau; a catch means you will get a husband within the year.

Put a pea pod with nine peas over the door. If a married man comes under it first, you will not be married within the year; if a single man, you will be married.

If you fall upstairs, you will not be married within the year.

Eat the point of a piece of pie first and you will be an old maid.

If your stocking comes down, you will be an old maid.

If you look under the bed, you will never marry.

If anyone sweeps around you, you will never marry.

When two young girls sleep together for the first time, if they tie their big toes together and the string is broken in the night, the one who has the shortest piece of string will marry first.

The white spots on your nails tell how many lovers you will have.

If you splash water on yourself while washing clothes, you will get a drunken husband.

If you cannot make a good fire, you will not get a good husband.

Here's a warning for the bride-to-be:

Change your name and not the letter,
Change for the worse and not the better.

If you go bare-footed, this rhyme may be useful:

Stub your toe, kiss your thumb,
Kiss your beau before one.

Walk around a wheat field on the first day of May and you will meet your mate.

Put a slice of wedding cake under your pillow for seven nights, and the seventh night you will dream of your future husband.

If a black cat takes up its home at a house, the unmarried daughters will have a good chance to marry.

If a bride wears another girl's garter when she is married, the girl will be married within the year.

The number of nails in the horseshoe which you pick up will be the number of years until you are married.

On Hallowe'en if you can eat an apple that is suspended on a string from the ceiling, you will marry within the year.

As many candles as are left on the birthcake after you blow once, that many years it will be till you are married.

On the first day of May, look in a well, and you will see the face of your future husband.

If you can blow the down from the dandelion in one blow, you will get the wish you make.

If two persons who think of the same thing at the same time hook their little fingers together and make a wish, the wish will come true.

If you see the new moon over your right shoulder and make a wish, the wish will come true.

When you find a four-leaf clover, swallow it and make a wish, and the wish will come true.

A wish made in a bed never before slept in will come true.

Sleep with the Bible under your head for three nights in a row, and you will dream of your future husband.

When you see the first star at night, say:

> Starlight, starbright,
> First star I see tonight,
> Wish I may, wish I might
> Have the wish I wish tonight.

Make a wish while putting a ring on another person's finger, at the same time stating how long the ring is to stay on. If the ring is not removed during that time, the wish will come true.

When two persons pull the wishbone of the chicken, the one who gets the larger part gets the wish.

Hang a wishbone over the front door, and the first man who passes under it is the man you will marry.

When you have put on a garment wrong side out, make a wish and it will come true.

Save the tip end of the pie, make a wish as you eat it, and the wish will come true.

When your dress skirt is turned up, spit on it and make a wish, and the wish will come true.

If a pregnant woman passes her hands over her body, she will give the baby a birthmark.

A woman in labor should hold salt between her hands.

Put sugar on the window to make the baby come.

If a baby loses its shoe, it will be rich.

Carry a new-born baby downstairs before it is carried upstairs so that it will have success in life.

The number of wrinkles on your forehead indicate the number of children you will have.

If a baby's fist does not close over money which is placed in its hand, it will always be poor.

If the hand of a new-born baby be open, it will have a generous disposition. If it is closed, it will be stingy.

If you see a man leading a horse with a side-saddle on Sunday, it is sure there will be a birth in that neighborhood within the week.

Your baby will resemble the person to whom you first carry it.

In time of war there will be more boys born than girls.

When a new-born child is veiled, it will have the gift of second sight.

If anyone steps over a baby, it will not grow for a year.

A child born on Christmas day can understand the speech of animals.

You have a right to kiss a girl when she makes a face at you.

Kiss a girl when you find her under the mistletoe.

Kiss a girl when you find her under the wishbone of a chicken.

Pare an apple in a single long strip, throw the peeling over your left shoulder, and it will form the initial of the first name of the person whom you will marry.

Burn the match to the end, and it will make the initial of the first name of the man you are to marry.

When you hear the first robin sing in the spring, sit down on a rock and take off your left stocking. If there is a hair in it, your sweetheart will call on you soon.

If you take the last piece of bread off the plate when it is not offered, you will never be married, but if you take it when it is offered, you will marry well.

When your shoe is untied, someone is thinking of your love.

If your thumbs turn back at the end, you will be a good housekeeper.

Shut your fist over your thumb for good luck.

To cross your legs when playing cards will bring good luck.

Sleep on mustard seeds, and witches cannot bother you.

For good luck, eat pancakes on Shrove Tuesday.

If a horse is restless in the morning, witches have been riding it in the night.

When a person sneezes, say "God bless you," and it will bring good luck.

Witchcraft
❖❖❖❖❖❖❖❖❖❖❖

For over a period of a half century I have recorded traditional stories of various kinds in West Virginia. In my boyhood I heard many stories of witches and ghosts. Among the people in the community where I grew up there was a strong belief in the reality of the supernatural. Anything out of the ordinary was likely to be accepted as a spiritual manifestation, or a warning of some dire event to happen. There were numerous warnings of death, and messages from the spiritual world were common. This attitude was not a result of ignorance, but a sign of the peoples' strong faith in God, who had many mysterious ways of informing people how to live. After all, if spirits communicated with living mortals in biblical times, could they not do the same today?

People firmly believed that the devil was still active and diligently striving to win souls away from God. Witches are people who have denied God and have sold themselves to the devil for his service; therefore, the belief in witchcraft could be no sin. Becoming a witch, however, was the unforgiveable sin.

The belief that certain people had the God-given power to break the spells of witches was also in keeping with the religion of the people. The belief in the existence of fairies, who could dispel the harm done by witches, was not accepted by the mountain people, who believed that good could come only from God. In European folklore, fairies were benevolent spirits who came from another world, not from heaven. The puritan influence in England had already banned the belief in fairies, and that influence was strong in America.

In my many years of collecting folklore in West Virginia, I found that most elderly people who sang traditional songs also knew many traditional tales that had been handed down from earlier generations. I was given clues by many people, especially by students in my extension classes in various parts of the state, which led me to folk singers. Whenever I first visited an elderly person, I would make it known that I was trying to write down or put on the tape recorder, stories that had been told of interesting things that had happened, especially stories of strange happenings. People often were hesitant about telling stories of witches and ghosts for fear of being scoffed at by the listener. To many, for several reasons, the subject of witchcraft was almost a forbidden one. The person hearing the story might be tempted to try the black art, especially if the story revealed the secret of how to become a witch. There was also fear that the story might stir the devil to do great harm, for, as one man said, "I tell you, the devil is still around, trying to draw people away from the Lord." Another deterrent was the fact that some of the witches in the stories had descendants who would be offended if the stories became known. One woman asked me, "If you were one of these descendants, how would you like for people to say to you, 'I hear that your grandma was a witch?'" Only by promising to keep the names of the witches secret, and in some instances not to reveal the name of the story-teller, could I hear the story.

We present these witch tales which we have found in West Virginia, simply as entertaining folk tales that have been heard by fireside listeners for many generations. We have no desire to influence anyone's belief in supernatural manifestations, but only suggest that the reader suspend his disbelief for a little time, as the poet Coleridge suggested to the readers of his poetry, and live temporarily in the story-book land of the imagination.

Of the many beliefs concerning witchcraft which we have found, all are to be found in the earliest accounts of witchcraft in various other lands. There is nothing new to be found in witchcraft in the region of the West Virginia hills. However, some of the beliefs concerning the power and activities of witches found in England, Scotland, and on the continent, and even in Salem, Massachusetts, are not found in West Virginia. For example, I have never heard any mention of the meeting of the witches, called "The Witches' Sabbath," when the witches gather on regular nights under the presidency of the devil to perform their black rites and reaffirm their subservience to the demon master. This witches' sabbath is well described by Nathaniel Hawthorne in his story, "Young Goodman Brown." I have never found any mention of the belief that witches can control the weather, such as causing hail to fall by dipping branches in water and then flinging them in the air.

One universal belief is that to become a witch one must follow a certain ritual in calling the devil forth, and then one must sign a compact with the devil so that the devil will give the mortal a servant to be with him to the end of his days on earth, at the end of which time the devil will claim his victim. We have found some very interesting variations of this ritual.

For example, one must go to the top of the highest mountain just at sunset, taking his rifle along, and just as the sun is setting over the horizon, he must turn around three times, each time swearing against the divinity and shooting his rifle at the setting sun. He must do this on three consecutive evenings. On the third evening, after the ceremony is completed, the devil will appear with his big book and his iron pen. Then the mortal must sign his name in his own blood, to make the compact with the devil. The time of the agreement may vary in number of years, but in most instances the mortal is not informed as to how long he will live. The compact stipulates that the devil will serve the mortal as long as he lives, but at the end of his earthly life the devil will take him off, body and soul, to hell.

Another variation of the ritual is that one must take a part of each of his fingernails, a part of each of his toenails, a little bit of skin cut from his body, a bit of his hair, and some prized possession. Just at midnight, these objects must be placed in a coal shovel and roasted over a fire. While these objects are roasting, the person must swear against the divinity. When they have burned away to ashes, the devil will appear with loud cries and noises like the rattling of chains. In this case, as in all other forms of the ritual, an important part of the ceremony is the abjuration of God the Father, God the Son, and God the Holy Ghost. And finally one must sign the compact which makes the devil his servant as long the mortal shall live on earth, at the end of which time the devil will take him to hell.

Another interesting form of the ritual is this: Anyone who wishes to become a witch may do so by going to one who is already a witch. There was a certain old woman who had been a witch for years. She took the convert, who was a young woman about twenty years old, to an old spring in the north side of a mountain. She took a large handkerchief and spread it out on the water. Then she tied a knot in each of three corners of the handkerchief, at the same time denouncing God the Father, God the Son, and God the Holy Ghost, while sprinkling some water on the convert. This was done three times until there were three knots, one in each of three corners of the handkerchief. Then the convert held the free corner, the one which was not knotted, and in her right hand she held the handkerchief and turned around three times, at the same time calling upon the devil to appear. When the devil appeared, he had a big book and an iron pen. It was necessary for the convert to draw some blood from her arm and sign her name in the book in her own blood. She then became a witch.

Still another way to become a witch is to take your rifle to the top of the highest mountain just as the full moon appears over the horizon. Shoot your rifle at the rising full moon three times, each time swearing against God. Do this on three consecutive nights. On the third night the devil will appear with his book and pen with which you must sign your name in the book in your own blood. The devil will then serve you as long as you live on earth, at the end of which time he will take you, body and soul, to hell.

I have recorded other variations of the ritual, but they all follow the same general pattern. First, there is the abjuration, the swearing against the divinity; second is the mysterious symbolic ritual to call the devil; and third, is the signing of the compact in blood.

Certain beliefs concerning the identity of witches are fairly universal. Some of these we have found in West Virginia. It is believed that a witch will have a mark on the body, often hidden, sometimes in the armpit, sometimes under the hair. A witch will have a certain look in the eyes called the evil eye, by means of which a spell can be cast on whomever the witch chooses to bewitch. The witch can cast spells on people to make them ill, even to cause death, and can cast spells on animals to make them ill or to make them useless. A witch can cast a spell on a hunter's gun so that it will not shoot straight. The witch can makes things appear suddenly where there was nothing before. She can hang up a rag and get milk from it, while at the same time her neighbors' cows will go dry. The witch can transform herself, or himself, and other people into various kinds of animals, usually a black cat. I have not heard of any specific modes of transportation used by witches. They simply move about and appear at different places suddenly and mysteriously. I have not heard any story in which a witch rides a broom.

In re-telling the witch tales as they were told to me, I have omitted names in many of them, or have substituted fictitious names. As the lady who told the story of "Uncle Johnnie" said to me: "I haven't told you his name, and I don't think I should, for he has relatives still living over here." In some stories we have given the names of the victims of witchcraft, but we believe it is better not reveal the identity of the witches.

THE WHITE ART

There are certain people who are said to be gifted with powers to do things which ordinary people cannot perform.

They have the power of healing, of finding underground water, of finding lost articles, of prophesying, and of communicating with the spiritual world. This power to perform beneficent acts is sometimes called the "white art;" it has nothing in common with the "black art," the name given to witchcraft. The white art is considered to be a special gift from God. A baby born with a veil, the term given to the fetal caul, over its face is supposed to have the power of prophecy. A posthumous child, one born after the death of its father, is said to have the power to cure certain ills and to prophesy. The seventh son of a seventh son has unusual powers, such as the power to prophesy and to heal the sick. However, any person who has great faith may be capable of healing illness or stopping blood by means of prayer. The belief in the efficacy of prayer is, of course, religion, but sometimes religion and superstition are confused. For example, many people believe that one with great faith can stop bleeding by reciting the "blood verse" in the Bible,—the sixth verse of the sixteenth chapter of Ezekiel. This belief in the efficacy of prayer is a manifestation of the person's religious faith. But when one insists that a man must not tell another man what the passage is, nor must a woman tell another woman, or the saying of the biblical passage will not be effective, it becomes superstition.

The practice of locating underground water, often called "water witching," has been common among people all over the world since ancient times. Even today it is a fairly common practice in all parts of rural America. I would like to share my own experience with this practice.

When my country home was built, I had a water well drilled by a competent driller. I told him where I wanted the well located so that it would be convenient for piping the water into the house. He drilled to a depth of two hundred and fifteen feet, but found very little water. A year later I secured the services of another well driller, hoping he might find a better supply of water, although I was not aware of his method of locating underground water. This man came with a peach fork and began to walk about the premises not far from the house. He held the peach fork by both of his hands, so that the butt end extended in front of him and parallel to the ground. He found three or four locations where the butt end of the fork bent down toward the ground, but one of the locations seemed to attract it more than the others. That is where he drilled, and at a depth of one hundred feet he found an abundance of water, which has to date supplied my household with water for seven years without fail.

I asked the gentleman if he thought anyone could find water with his forked stick. He said, "No, only certain people." He then showed me how to hold the fork so that I could try it to find out whether I was one who could do it. Imagine my amazement when I felt the butt end of the fork pulling toward the ground just as it had in his hands. Later, I cut two pieces of coat hanger wire about two feet long each and bent them into a ninety-degree angle. I held one wire in each hand so that one side of the angle was perpendicular, while the other pointed forward horizontally. When I passed over the locations where the peach fork had reacted, the wires turned inward to touch each other. My son, who is a professor of physics in a well-known college, scoffed at the practice, but when he tried it and got the same results, he had no scientific explanation.

A fifty-three page booklet entitled *The Divining Rod—A History of Water Witching,* by Arthur J. Ellis, was published by the United States Department of the Interior, Government Printing Office, Washington, D. C., in 1938. It contains a bibliography of more than five hundred printed sources of information, dated from the sixteenth century to the twentieth century, on the subject of "water witching."

Another power that some people were reputed to possess was the ability to break spells that had been cast by witches. This was not a God-given power, but one that was acquired by learning it from another person who knew the secret of the power. These people were called "witch doctors." The reader will find several instances among the following stories in which the spell of the witch was broken by the witch doctor. In some cases the witch doctor, after performing the act which breaks the spell of the witch, "murmurs some strange words," so that the spell of the witch cannot return. The words are always unintelligible to any listener, and no one has ever tried to explain them to me.

UNCLE JOHNNIE BEWITCHES THE COWS

It is unusual for a man to be a witch; almost all of the witches in the stories we have recorded are women. However, I have heard many stories about the old witch man known as "Uncle Johnnie," and of the mischievous things he did. I have never heard the term "warlock" used in any stories in West Virginia. One summer I sat on the porch with Mrs. Robert Pettry in Raleigh County and listened to her stories about Uncle Johnnie and other witches. In telling this story, she uses the word "funny" to mean strange. When she says, "We thought it was funny," she means "We thought it was strange." Here is the story in her own words.

This old man called Uncle Johnnie came to my Aunt Eliza Morris and wanted to borrow one of her churns. He said, "Lize, I want to get one of your churns."

And she said, "Now, Uncle Johnnie, I'm afraid to let you—I can't let you have that churn. I've only got two, and I have to churn every day. I get so much milk, and I've got to keep my cream in one ready to churn the next day, and keep my buttermilk in the other."

Well, he went off in a huff. He said, "All right, madam, all right. You can drink your milk, but I'll eat your butter."

Well, she said her husband had hewed out a nice bowl, a big concern, and she said that when she took her butter off there was so much of it that she gave it to neighbors and used it for cooking and all purposes. So that evening when he went off, she started churning. As usual, she got everything ready, and she said she churned two long hours, but no butter. She said just foam would come on that milk, and finally she just set it aside.

Well, it went on that way for about a week. She said her geese would come up just dancing like women and carrying on terrible. And the cows at last just began to give bloody milk. She never used the milk any more after that, but she'd milk it and give it to the hogs.

So her husband went to an old man named Jimmie Webb. Now he was supposed to take the witch spell off of things. And when her husband went up there and told Uncle Jimmie Webb what had happened, he said, "Now you go home and tell Lize to milk tonight and in the morning, and set the milk where it will get thick as usual, and I'll come down tomorrow evening and churn for her."

Well, she said that about four-thirty or five in the evening she looked, and here came this old man walking on his cane, and he had nine hickory switches in under his arm. And he says, "Lize, I've come down to churn for you."

She said she got him a cloth and spread it over his lap, and set the churn out on the little porch. And she said he'd begin this churning—he'd churn with his left hand and he'd whip the churn with one of those switches in his right hand. She said he'd whip one switch up, and he'd lay it aside and get another one, until he'd whipped all nine of those switches up on that churn. And she said she never saw such an amount of butter that there was in that one churning of milk.

And he said, "Now, Lize, what I've done won't be worth anything if you lend them anything off this place. It won't be long now till they'll come here to borrow something."

Well, she said it wasn't but just about half an hour before here came one of the girls. She came running, and she said, "Pap hurt his back awful bad. He wants to borrow some turpentine." They didn't have many doctors then, and all families kept simple remedies like turpentine, castor oil, and things like that. She had to refuse him. She said, "I'm sorry, but I don't have the turpentine."

When Uncle Jimmie Webb had finished the churning he went around every cow and murmured something. And he said, "Now, I don't think you'll have any more trouble." And she didn't. But this is the part of the story that I thought was funny.

There was an old man that lived down at Horse Creek, and he and his brother, who was my first husband's father, they owned a lot of land that extended out to a mountain that was called Cherry Pine Mountain, and they were having a log-rolling. They didn't realize the value of a big poplar tree then—the ground was all they cared for—and they would cut these big trees down and burn them. Maybe they'd saw out some wood, and then make fences. They'd just roll the trees down and make fences. They had a big gathering of men working, and this old Uncle Johnnie was there. The man who was telling this said that they had done a wonderful day's work and had a big field cleared up.

And the man said, "Now, you've done an awful good day's work, and we certainly appreciate it. Now, we'll roll these logs down, and then we'll go and eat supper."

The men had their cant hooks under the logs, a-prising in under the logs. He said that all of a sudden this old Uncle Johnnie that I've told you about, gave a big scream and leaped in the air. He didn't have any undershirt on, just a faded cotton shirt, and when he commenced screaming and writhing like someone in agony, they could see the white welts through that shirt—just bloody welts all over his back. And he said they had to carry him out of there. And he said, "I never did know what caused that, but I never saw a man suffer so in my life."

Now this man who told this didn't know anything about the churn and how Uncle Jimmie Webb had whipped the spell off. But of course we know what caused the welts. It happened just as Uncle Jimmie was whipping the churn.

UNCLE JOHNNIE FRIGHTENS MRS. DICKENS

Uncle Johnnie, the witch man, was known to play pranks on people, sometimes for malice, but more often for fun. Will Dickens knew Uncle Johnnie and could tell many stories about him. I sat on the porch with Mr. Dickens in Raleigh County in the summer of 1960 and heard him tell how Uncle Johnnie frightened Mrs. Dickens with snakes.

My wife wanted to go out and pick some beans. It was along in September, and I was a-cuttin' my corn and takin' care of the fodder. When my wife started up the hill, the old man, Uncle Johnnie, said, "Don't you go up there. Somethin' will ketch ye." He was a-settin' on the porch thar, and they's a big rock at the foot of the hill. When she went to pass that rock pile and wasn't a-listenin' to him, the snakes got to jumpin' outa that pile of rocks, just a-pokin' their heads out and a-lickin' their tongues. I heerd her scream, and I went to her. Buddy, she throwed down her basket and the sack she had in the basket, and she run down home, and him just a-sittin' there. It was an awful hot day, and me and my dad went up and moved that rock pile. We took us a gun to kill the snakes, and we was about three hours a-movin' that rock pile. And they wasn't a blessed thing in there but just a few little bugs like them that stays in the ground. My dad was mad, and he was a-gonna cut him up with an axe. "Well," the old man said, "You'll get into something worse than that."

DEATH AND BURIAL OF UNCLE JOHNNIE

The following story is another I heard about Uncle Johnnie from Will Dickens.

Well, the old man died in a few days. Johnnie Dickens, my brother, why he made caskets all the time—home-made caskets. And he always took a stick and measured the man and then measured the casket. And he forgot that measurin' stick, as he called it, and left it in the barn. When we hauled the old man off to the grave to bury him, we started down the road with him. My brother had a good mule team. And we got right to the mouth of the creek down here where there is a little ford there. Well, that wagon just began to mash down. There wasn't nothin' but just a little gravel in that creek, and the water wasn't over a foot deep. And them mules couldn't pull that wagon across the creek. My brother called on them three or four times, but they couldn't move it. My brother is pretty wicked, and he said, "The old —— — — ——, he's always been a witch. I'm gonna throw him out in there!"

And me and Bird Dickens and him started to pick up the casket and roll 'er out, and them mules just started up and never gave us any more trouble. He's buried right down there. (Mr. Dickens pointed to a small graveyard not far down the road.)

When we got back, my brother that made the casket, said, "I forgot that measurin' stick out in the barn." He went out and got it and throwed it under a patch of brush. The next mornin' when he got up, there a-settin' on the porch beside the door was that measurin' stick. And he jumped on the boy, Grady Dickens, and he said, "How come you to bring that measurin' stick back after I throwed it away?" The boy said, "I never saw it, Dad. I didn't know you'd throwed it away." And he throwed it away again, and the next day it was back a-settin' beside the door. And he took that measurin' stick and said, "I will get shed of it." And he took it up this crooked holler, and took it by the end and just throwed as far as he could throw it. When he got back, there set his measurin' stick. And he took it up to the head of the holler where he was a-diggin' his coal and shot it down with dynamite. That's all the way he could get shed of it.

THE BLACK CAT MURDERS

Narrators of folk tales, especially tales of witches or ghosts, usually begin with the statement that the story they are about to tell is true. They even give names of people and places.

Mrs. Robert Pettry, the woman who told the story of how Uncle Johnnie put the spell on the cows, told me the story of the girl who became a black cat. She prefaced her story by saying: "I don't know if you'd be interested in this story or not. Now, the woman who told me this didn't tell it for the truth, and I'm not telling it to you for the truth. But it was a legend, and where it took place, I don't even know." She then began her story:

There was a man who lived in a big city and was wealthy, but he invested and loaned money, and he went bankrupt. But while he had this money, he had bought thousands of acres of timberland just to keep from paying taxes on his money. After he lost his money by investments, he told his wife and daughter—they had only the one girl, who was in society and had all kinds of jewelry and things—"We've got to sell all this to pay the creditors. There's only one show for us," he said. "I might regain some of my losses by that timberland that I have. If we can get a mill and go out there and stay, I might get back on my feet again."

The girl didn't like the idea, and she fought against it; oh, she just fought bitterly. But he went ahead and sold her furs and jewelry, and got pretty well out of debt. Then he bought a big sawmill and got a crew of men, and they went to work cutting the timber. Then he built a nice bungalow for himself, his wife and daughter. At the mill, which was just a little piece below the house, he built a shanty for the watchman to stay in. The slabs and the fall-off from the timber had to be burned every night to keep them out of the way, and there had to be a watchman there so that he would have the fire going and have the mill in operation for the next day.

One morning he went down to see why the fire hadn't been built, and he found the watchman lying there with his throat cut, just like somebody had cut it all to pieces, and the watchman was dead.

Well, he got another man, and the same thing happened to him. He didn't want to have any more men killed like that, and that mill was idled. One evening a man came along leading a pet bear. Now, when I was a child, every year at our one-room school there used to be a man a-comin' through leadin' a pet bear. And my father would keep them overnight, for he had a rather nice home down the road there, and my father would keep almost everyone who passed that way at night.

This man that had the bear asked to stay overnight at the house of the man who owned the sawmill. He said, "Well, I've not got any room in my house at all for you to stay, but I have a house down there at my sawmill with a good bed in it and plenty to eat, but I'm not sure you want to stay there." Then he told him what had happened to these two other men who had been killed, and said, "I've not asked anybody to stay there since the last one was killed." The man patted his bear on the head and said to him, "We're not afraid, are we, Fido?" And the bear growled and nudged up against him. It was just a regular pet.

He took the man down there and showed him where the things were to cook, and showed him the bed things, and said, "Now don't you let anybody in here tonight. Now you lock the door, and even if I come, don't you let me in here."

The next morning he went down, and the man opened the door. He had his breakfast ready and everything seemed normal. But the man told him what had happened in the night. He said he was sitting there after he ate his supper and had fed the bear, and he was so tired, he said he dozed off to sleep before he went to bed. He said the bear was lying there at his feet, when he heard a little rattling sound at the door. And through the keyhole of that door came a long black cat. It just leaped right in, and when it got close to him it just gave a great big squall and grabbed him by the throat, and he said it had him almost dead before he could even breathe. And he just had enough strength to tell his bear, "Sic him, Fido." When he did that, he said that the bear gave a big leap and grabbed off the left paw of this cat, and when it fell to the floor it was a girl's hand and had a ring on it. And he said she went out the door screaming like a woman, and went right through the keyhole. He said that the blood was all over the place.

He said he took the hand up and wrapped it up in a piece of paper, and said he was never bothered any more that night after he lay down and went to sleep. When the owner knocked at the door the next morning, he saw that he was really surprised. And when the owner asked him, "Did anything happen here last night?" He said, "Yes, a little." Then he showed him the hand that he'd wrapped up in paper. He held it out and the man fell back. He said, "My Lord, that's my daughter's hand. She told me that this mill would never do me any good, and it hasn't so far." He said, "She's sick in bed this morning. You come and go with me."

They went up to the house, and when the man went in he reached out and got a rifle. He said, "You come on in here in the bedroom." He went in there, and the girl was lying there —very pretty—and she had the cover pulled up around her chin. Her father said to her, "Hold out your hand and let me see what's wrong with you." And she put out her right hand; she wouldn't hold out the left one. And he forced her. He took the cover and pulled it down so that they could see that her left hand had been chewed off. Then her father shot her. Of course, that was all he could do, for she had given herself to the devil to become a witch to get back at her father for making her live out there in the woods away from her friends of the city society.

THE WITCH OF BOOGER HOLE

One of the most interesting witch stories I have ever found had its origin in Clay County, West Virginia, on Big Otter Creek, at a community which was once known as "Booger Hole." The story was told to me by the grand-daughter-in-law of the woman who was said to be a witch. In the story, the witch woman is simply called "Grandma."

It was back about the beginning of the century that Grandma lived at a place called "Booger Hole" on Big Otter

Creek. Grandma had a mare that she called "Old Fannie." One day a young fellow named Andrew came to Grandma and said, "I'd like to borrow your mare to do a little plowing." Grandma said, "All right, Andrew, you can use her if you don't work her too hard and be sure to feed her well."

Well, after three days Andrew fetched Old Fannie back, and when Grandma looked at her, she said, "Andrew, you've ruined my mare. You worked her too hard, and she looks mighty peaked. Now, Andrew, I'm a-gonna ride you every night till you're just as peaked as Old Fannie."

Well, some folks around said that Grandma was a witch, and that she could do strange things. I don't think Grandma ever witched anyone—but then, she might a-done it. Anyhow, Andrew said that she came in of a night and put a bridle on him and rode him all over Pilot Knob. He'd wake up in the morning all tired out, with burrs in his hair, and his mouth sore from the bridle bit. This went on till Andrew was almost crazy.

Grandma lived in a little log house that had been used at one time as a schoolhouse. It didn't have lights (glass) in the windows, but Grandma kept a quilt hanging over the window at night. One night someone raised the quilt and shot poor old Grandma as she was a-settin' in a chair. I went in there right after she was shot, and I saw Grandma with her arms a-hangin' down over the sides of the chair, and the blood a-runnin' down.

Well, they accused Andrew of the murder, and they arrested him. But they didn't have any evidence against him, only that they said Grandma had put a spell on him. So they let Andrew go.

Now there's another part to the story that some folks don't know about. There was a man who had come to this community, whose name was Henry Hargiss. He was a stonemason, and he built chimneys for a lot of folks around here. People said he kept money around him all the time, for a lot of folks didn't trust the banks to keep their money. Henry Hargiss disappeared, and nobody seemed to know what had become of him, though a lot of folks thought there had been foul play somewhere. Grandma thought she knowed one of the men who had killed Henry Hargiss, so they say she put a spell on this man's horse so that he couldn't ketch it in the field. The horse had always been tame, but now every time the man would come near it, it would kick and bite. He had an idea that Grandma had put a spell on his horse, so he went to her and begged her to take the spell off his horse. She said, "All right. I'll take the spell off your horse if you'll tell me where Henry Hargiss is buried." Well, he finally told her.

It was not long after that when we were in a room. There was Grandma and some other women, and I was there with my little baby. I had been married the year before to Grandma's grandson, and I was holding my little baby in my arms. Grandma said, "I could light my pipe, (she always smoked a clay pipe), and before it goes out I could take you to where Henry Hargiss is buried." I tried to get Grandma to keep still, but these women had already heard her. Well, it was not long after that when they shot poor old Grandma. And I always did believe that these women told their husbands that Grandma knew too much, and that's why they killed her.

THE SAD DEATH OF MARY FISHER

Aunt Mary Gainer Wilson, who lived at Tanner, Gilmer County, who sang many songs and told stories for me, one day in 1930 told me this unusual witch story.

Young Mary Fisher, was about seventeen at the time, and she and her mother were sitting in the front room of their home. Mrs. Fisher looked out the door and saw an old woman approaching the house. "Mary," said Mrs. Fisher, "There comes that old witch. Now if she comes in the house, don't let her pick up anything and carry it away with her, for if she does, she can put a spell on us."

When the old woman came to the door, Mrs. Fisher told her, "Now we don't want you to come in this house, for you're a

witch, and everybody knows it." Lots of people had said that
they knew this old woman could do strange things, and they
were pretty sure she was a witch. Well, the old woman was
insulted. She walked right down the path by the garden, leaned
over the fence, and picked a leaf of lettuce from a lettuce bed
that Mary Fisher had planted. The old woman turned to them
with the lettuce leaf in her hand, waving it and laughing.

It was only a short time till Mary Fisher got sick and began
to waste away. They knew that she had been put under the spell
by that old witch woman. They got a witch doctor, who tried
various cures, but he couldn't do anything for her, and she
faded away and died.

Mary was a good singer, and she sang quite a bit. She had an
instrument with three strings that she sometimes played. The
song that she sang most in the last days before she died was
"What Shall I Give To Thee?" Mary had a big shepherd dog that
used to lie at her feet, but when she sang this song, the dog
would be disturbed and would run around her. This is the song
she sang:

THE WITCH DOCTOR'S SILVER BULLET

Mrs. Robert Pettry of Raleigh County, who told this story said she knew it to be true, because she knew the people.

I lived by an old woman who said she was bewitched. Her son lived right below me in a house, and when my husband would be away working at night, this old woman would come and stay with me. Her name was Sarah, and she had this oldest son before she was married, and she lived with him. She said that there was a woman who lived up on Clear Creek who got jealous of her. And she said that when she was in bed with this baby, when it was born, she said that she could see this woman coming in, but her mother couldn't see her. She said she'd come right through the keyhole of the door, and she'd stick pins in this baby, and the blood would come out. She'd just do things to get even with her.

Well, her daddy went to an old witch doctor that lived up there above Talcourt. When he came in he asked for bullet molds. People had those old rifles, and they used bullet molds to mold the bullets. And he had a package of needles in his pocket. She said he took out nine needles and broke the point off one of those needles. And he said, "I'd like to have a big piece of cardboard." They had a great big log house, and they burned wood in the fireplace.

This old man who was a witch doctor got the pasteboard and drew a picture of a woman, making the toes and all. He said, "We don't want to hurt her too bad. I think I'll just shoot off one of her toes." He said, "That'll stop her from doing these crazy things." You know, this witch would pinch the baby and do all kinds of things, but her mother, her father, and her sisters couldn't see her. So, this old man took her picture and nailed it up on a big oak tree in the yard. Then he stepped back a pace and took the rifle and shot the big toe off of the right foot.

And he said, "Now they'll be here to borrow something

before long." Well, sure enough, they came to borrow turpentine. They said this old woman was chopping wood and cut the end of her big toe off, and they wanted the turpentine. They said they didn't let her have the turpentine.

THE VIOLENT WITCH

In most of the witch stories which I have recorded, the witch doctor is able to take the spell off the victim before death occurs. Mrs. Robert Pettry, who told this story, was sure that it was true, for all of the people were known to her grandmother.

John Jerrold down here, who died a few years back, had two sons. My grandmother told me this. There was an old woman got mad at them, because she was always borrowing things from them, and finally they quit letting her have things, because she would never bring anything back that she had borrowed. Well, my grandmother said that this old woman would come through the keyhole of the door with a hammer, and she beat one of the boys with that hammer till he finally died with the blood gushing out of his ears and his mouth. Even when they stopped the keyhole up, she would push through it and attack this boy. Finally the father made a silver bullet, and he went to that old woman and showed her the bullet.

He said to her, "Now we know you're a witch, and you've caused the death of our boy. I'm a-telling you right now, if you ever do anything more to any of my family, I'm a-gonna kill you with this silver bullet."

And she begged him not to hurt her, and she promised him that she would never do anything to harm anybody. My grandmother knew this woman, and she knew her to do strange things. But this took place before I was born, and I'm telling it to you just as my grandmother told it to me. But grandmother *knew* her to do things like that.

THE WITCH OF BUCK RUN

Mrs. Eugenia Roberts, was one of my students in folk-
lore in an extension class at Parkersburg in 1950. Mrs. Roberts
was from Wirt County. She told me the stories about Mary
Leadum of Tyler County. Mrs. Roberts said her grandfather
told her about Mary, who lived almost a century ago.

Mrs. Leadum was a stooped and crippled old lady. One
could always hear her coming by the "tap, tap, tap, of her cane
as she walked along the country road. Her back had been
broken in an accident when she was a girl. People thought she
was strange, which gave rise to the stories in the neighborhood
that Mary was a witch. She was a frequent visitor in the Taylor
family home.

The good yellow cream of the Taylor's cows had for years
been churned into butter and traded at the village store for the
weekly supply of groceries. One day, after Mary Leadum had
visited at the Taylor home, one of the girls got the churn ready
and began to churn. She churned for about an hour, and still
there was no sign of butter. No matter how hard she churned,
the butter would not come. This was a very serious thing for the
Taylor family, for they depended on the butter to trade at the
store.

Word got around very soon among the neighbors that the
Taylors couldn't get butter from their cream. Since the trouble
started right after Mary Leadum had been there, they were
pretty sure that she had put a spell on the cream so that no
butter would come. One of the neighbors suggested that they
break the spell by heating a butcher knife until it was red hot,
and then plunging it into the churning of cream. She said this
would break the spell. And when they had done this, a visitor
would soon come and want to borrow something. This visitor
would be the witch.

Friday morning was the time to churn, so that the fresh butter could be taken to the store on Saturday. As usual, the cream

would not turn into butter. The butcher knife was then heated to a cherry red and thrust in the churn of cream. Only a little more churning was necessary to produce the usual large amount of butter.

"Tap, tap, tap," sounded on the boardwalk leading up to the house. There was the bent figure of Mary Leadum.

"Mrs. Taylor, could you loan me a teaspoon of baking soda?" asked Mary Leadum. "I've a burn on my leg and would like to put some soda on it." And there on her leg was a large red welt in the exact image of a butcher knife.

THE WITCHERY OF MARY LEADUM

Mrs. Roberts had another story about the woman who was thought to be a witch, Mary Leadum.

There was a young farm couple who lived on Short Run, in Tyler County, West Virginia. Since both of them worked out in the field together quite often, they had to have someone to take care of their only child, a little baby girl. They hired Mary Leadum to stay in the house to take care of the baby and to do some light housework. One day the couple went out in the field, leaving the baby in its little bed sleeping peacefully with Mary Leadum looking after her. They hadn't been in the field very long when Mary came screaming for them to come to the house. When they got to the house, they found their baby dead in her bed.

They accused Mary Leadum of being a witch and of putting a spell on the child so that it died. Of course, Mary denied it, but she was forced to leave. She was then taken in by another family to do housework. The father of this family said he didn't believe in witchcraft, and that he was not afraid of Mary Leadum.

Mary used to sit at her spinning wheel as the children gathered around watching her spin. But the biggest attraction was the little white mouse that would climb on top of the spinning wheel and sit there while Mary spun. Then it would disappear mysteriously. No one seemed to know where it came from, but it was thought to be a result of the witchery of Mary Leadum.

THE MYSTERIOUS DOE

Witches are supposed to have the power to put a spell on a hunter's gun so that it will not shoot straight. There was a time when there was a lot of game in these woods, and some people depended on hunting to supply their meat. They could sell the deer hide for a pretty good price and get enough money to buy things at the store, such as coffee, salt, and cotton goods.

Mrs. Lenore Danley, of Gilmer County, told me the story about a man who was a very good hunter.

Nobody could shoot a rifle better than John Stalnaker. But it got so that for some reason he could not shoot straight at all. In the evenings he would go out, and every time he went he would see a large doe. Try as he would, he could never hit it. There was an old woman who lived not far from his place, and lots of folks said they thought she was a witch. He was pretty sure that this old woman had put a spell on his rifle so that it wouldn't shoot straight. He made a silver bullet, and the next time he saw the doe, he shot at it and hit it in the leg. It ran, but he followed it by the trail of blood, and it led him right straight to the door of the old woman who was thought to be a witch. He knocked at the door, and one of the girls came to the door and told him that grandma had hurt her leg very bad and couldn't see anyone. He knew that this witch had turned herself into a doe, and when he shot the doe, he was really shooting the old woman. After that he had no trouble with his rifle.

A WITCH'S SPELL TAKEN OFF

The story of the widow Danby was contributed by Gale Miller, a student in folklore at Glenville State College in 1950.

When Jim Gates got married, he built himself a little house over there just above the mouth of Wildcat on land that his pa had given him, and Jim and his wife moved in there. Old widow Danby and her daughter lived up the hollow a piece from where Jim lived. Well, they called her "Widow Danby," but actually she had this girl and was never married. Jim went with the girl for quite a while, and they say her mother wanted her to marry Jim. But Jim met this other girl, and it wasn't long till they got married.

Jim had always been a good hunter ever since he was just a small boy. They say his pa was a good hunter, and he taught Jim how to handle a rifle. Well, just a little while after Jim and his wife moved in there, Jim went out hunting, thinking he could get a deer for his wife. Jim said he saw at least five deer not very far from his house back on the ridge. One of them was so close that he said he knew he couldn't miss it, but he said he couldn't hit anything. Finally he came back home just a-rarin', and he said he knew that old woman up the holler had put a spell on his gun so it wouldn't hit anything. She didn't like it because he didn't marry her daughter.

Jim said, "I'll fix her." And he went up against the bank and got a hickory sapling and named it after the old woman. Then he twisted that sapling almost double. The next time he saw that old woman, she was bent over almost double. Jim had no more trouble with his rifle.

THE RACCOON WITCH

Although it is possible for a witch to transform herself into any kind of animal she chooses, it is very unusual to hear of one changing to a raccoon. In this story there seems to be no reason for Martha Pringle to become a raccoon except to plague the hunters. The reason for her doing this is not given in the story, which was told to me by Elmer Legg of Clay County, who heard it from an elderly woman.

Moll Lynch was talking to my sister and me one evening when we had called on her, because her husband was poorly and we wanted to ask if there was anything they wanted.

"I hear Lige Fisher's hound a-howlin' again tonight," she said. "And mind what I'm tellin' you, we'll hear some bad news. It's a bad omen to hear a dog howling like that at night. It reminds me of that black, windy night when I heard a strange hound a-howlin' on that ridge yonder. It was just about midnight. And the next morning, just as dawn was a-breakin', here came Anderson Pringle to get me to come to see his wife, Martha, who had taken sick during the night.

"Afterwards, I heard what had happened. That night George Heater took his dogs and went a-huntin'. The dogs treed a big coon. George shot at it, and he shot at it, but he couldn't kill the coon, and George is a good shot, too. So he got out a silver bullet he was a-carryin' in his pocket, put it in his gun and shot once more. This time the coon screamed like a woman, leaped from the tree, and ran like a hant. The dogs chased it a piece, but gave up and returned. And from that time on, Martha Pringle always had an injured side and never saw a well day."

THE WITCH'S FUNERAL

Back around the beginning of this century, a most mysterious event occurred at a cemetery in Barbour County, West Virginia. An elderly minister, whose father had been present at the funeral and had related the story many times to him, told me this story.

There was a woman living near Nestorville who was thought to be a witch. People said that they knew her to do many strange things. If she got mad at anyone, their cream wouldn't churn, their pigs would get sick, or some other bad things would happen to them. Finally the woman died. A grave was dug for her on the ridge, and a great procession of people attended the funeral, most of them likely coming out of curiosity. It was a beautiful clear day with the sun shining and not a cloud in the sky. A large crowd stood around the grave as the body was lowered into it. Suddenly there was a loud clap of thunder, and a streak of lightning struck the grave. Smoke and the smell of brimstone came from the grave.

When the smoke had cleared away, there was nothing in the grave. Both the casket and the body had been consumed. Not one of the people standing near the grave was harmed. That grave is still there and is still open. Weeds and vines have grown in the grave, and there is now a fence around it.

THE BEWITCHED PIGS

This story was told by an old gentleman who was ninety-two years old at the time. He firmly believed in witches, and was likely to attribute almost everything unpleasant that happened to him to some form of witchcraft. He told me he did not want his name published.

When I was a boy, my grandfather came to visit at our home. My mother went away for the day and left our grandfather with us boys. Before leaving, she asked the old man to feed the pigs. Now the old man was a lazy fellow, and didn't want to feed the pigs, but he finally did feed them. When mother returned home that evening, she found that the pigs had not eaten their morning feed, nor would they eat their evening feed. She decided immediately that the old man had cast a spell on the pigs so they wouldn't eat.

First thing she did, she went to the pig house and got some bristles from the pigs. Then she took those bristles in the house and burned them in the stove. This was supposed to break the spell, and it did. The pigs immediately ate both their morning and their evening feeding.

As soon as mother burned the bristles, the old man left the house and did not return all night. She wasn't too much alarmed, because he had often gone visiting at a neighbor's house and stayed all night. In the morning, some neighbors found the old man out in the woods asleep, and they brought him home. One side of his leg had been burned.

THE WITCH OF BULL RUN MEETS HER MATCH

This story was contributed by Lenore Danley, who was a student in my class in folklore at Glenville State College.

Old Aunt Eunice, a native of Bull Run, Gilmer County, was well known as a witch. She had sold herself to the devil when she was sixteen years old, and she said the devil promised her that she would live a hundred years after that. She was approximately one hundred and twenty when she died.

Aunt Eunice was able to make people's cows stop giving milk. She could take a hatchet and stick it in the corner of the house, steal a dishrag and hang it on the hatchet, and that evening the cows of the neighbors would give no milk.

One time Aunt Eunice bewitched Hezakiah Griffith, who lived on Crooked Run. Every night when Hezekiah went to bed, a darning needle would hop across the floor and jump on his chest. Finally he couldn't put up with it any more, so he went to the witch doctor to get a cure. The witch doctor told him to catch the needle and fetch it to him.

The next night he lay in bed and pretended to be asleep, but when the needle jumped on his chest he was ready for it. He grabbed that needle and held on to it, and early in the morning before daylight he took that needle to the witch doctor. The witch doctor heated the needle until it was red-hot, then he bent it double. He told Hezekiah not to let Aunt Eunice get hold of the needle.

Well, it wasn't long till she sent someone after him, and she said she wanted to see him right away. When he got to her house, he found her all doubled up with the cramps. She was bent just like that needle. She begged him to straighten out that needle. After she promised him that she wouldn't bother him any more, he put the needle in the fire to get it hot, and when he did this she moaned with pain. When he straightened out the needle, she got well right away. And Hezekiah was never bothered any more after that.

THE WITCH MAN OF CALHOUN COUNTY

This story was told by Mrs. Eugenia Roberts of Wirt County, who said that every bit is true.

I grew up in a small rural community. Almost ever since I can remember, we were told that an old man, who lived about three miles from our home, was a witch. He was an object of mingled curiosity and terror to us children. At night we were afraid, and nothing in the world could have taken us near the old man's place. But in the daytime we became braver, and we often talked of going to see him do some of the many strange things that people said he could do. We had heard that he could even make a table walk without touching it.

Finally, one bright spring afternoon, we set out just after Sunday dinner. Because we didn't want to be laughed at, or stopped from going, we told our folks that we were going after wild honeysuckle. There were eight of us, five girls and three boys, ranging in age from ten to fourteen.

It took us about an hour to walk the distance of three miles to the little plank house where the man and his wife lived alone. It seemed as if there could be no evil in this setting. The honeysuckle and the fruit trees were blooming around the house, and the door was open, letting the sunlight in. The old man himself stood in the door and welcomed us. He was slight of build, somewhat bent, and had curly white hair.

After we had all told him our names and something about our schoolwork, one of the boys asked him if he would make the table walk for us. He said, "Certainly I'll do it for you."

We stood near the door leading into a room which served as kitchen and dining room combined. It had a wood-burning stove and a large cupboard, and in the center of the room was a home-made table, with two home-made wooden benches. The old man moved the benches away from the table to the edge of the room. Then he came back to the doorway, crossed his hands, and looked down intently, mumbling something which we could not understand, and then raised his head. We saw the table begin to move about the room. It seemed to rise a few inches above the floor and glide about the room, almost as if there were wires attached and someone was guiding it. But there were no wires, and no one was touching the table. But there were eight frightened children watching as the old man, with a strange half-smile, looked down, muttered something again, and the table returned to its place and was still.

The old man asked us how we liked it, and one of the boys said it was all right, but he thought we ought to go back home.

But the old man said he would like us to see one more trick before we left. Then he took from his pocket an ordinary pocket knife and stuck it in one of the cracks in the wall, leaving the blade hanging loosely in the crack. Then taking a bucket of water from the kitchen stove, he hung the bucket on the handle of the knife, which supported the bucket, although it didn't seem possible.

We thanked the old man for showing us the tricks, and he asked us to come back again soon. We never did get up enough courage to visit him again.

Years passed, and the old man became very ill. He said that the devil was coming after him soon, because he had sold himself to the devil to become a witch. He would try to sleep, but he would rise up in his bed screaming that the devil was there, though no one could see anything unusual. They put a Bible under the old man's pillow, but he made them take it away, screaming that the devil would punish him for it. He finally died in terrible agony.

THE DEVIL TAKES HIS VICTIM

One summer evening I sat on the porch with an elderly couple, Mr. and Mrs. Homer Sampson, who lived in a small house located on a flat overlooking a wooded valley in Raleigh County, West Virginia. They had lived there for the entire time of their married life—fifty-three years. They talked of the years when their children were small, when they all gathered together in a circle to sing songs and tell stories. The stories were mostly of things that had happened to the parents in their younger days, some of them sad, some funny. It seemed to me that they were avoiding any reference to witchcraft, and I was somewhat reluctant to ask about it. I had found through long experience, that it was a subject that people would not talk about, either because they thought their listeners might scoff at

WITCHCRAFT 165

the stories, or because they considered it a dangerous subject.
Mrs. Sampson said, "I tell you, the devil is still around." When
I mentioned that I had heard stories of witches and had read
some stories which a friend of mine had written for the paper,
Mrs. Sampson said, "Yes, I saw one of the stories, and I cut it
out and put it in my Bible." By doing this, she explained, the
witch could not harm anyone.

"There was one witch I could tell you about," Mr. Sampson
said. "She's gone now, but I tell you, she did strange things, and
lots of folks were afraid of her."

"Did she claim to have the power?" I asked.

"Yes, she did," said Mr. Sampson. Here is the story he told me.

There was a young girl who said this old woman told her
how she could be a witch and do almost anything she wanted
to do, if she'd go with her to the top of the highest hill here and
do what the old woman told her to do. She told her they would
walk up to the top of the big rock there for three nights straight
when the moon was full, just at the time of night when the
moon was directly overhead. The girl would have to swear
against God each night. On the third night the devil would
come with a big book and an iron pen. The girl would have to
draw some blood from her arm and sign her name in the book.
She would then be a witch.

This girl told us about it. She told how she started up the hill
with the old woman, but she got scared and ran back home.
Right after that the girl got sick. Her father was sure the old
witch had put a spell on her. So he drew a picture of that old
woman and burnt it in the fire. The girl got well right soon, and
that old woman wasn't seen for quite a spell. Some folks who
went to her house said she'd spilled some hot lard and got a bad
burn. But I reckon you know what happened to her.

Well, I'm not sure I ought to tell you any more about her.
She's gone now, but some of her relatives are living around
here. But there's more that I could tell you. She got mad at
Lafe Perkins once, because Lafe wouldn't let her pick

blackberries in the patch above his house. It was an easy patch to get to, and Lafe said he wanted the berries for himself. She told him he'd be sorry. Well, they say Lafe was troubled by all kind of things after that. For a long time he couldn't sleep of a night. Sometimes he would hear an awful scream like a woman running around the house, and when he'd go to the door to see what it was, he saw a big black cat a-runnin' around the house a-screamin'. He kept all the doors and windows shut, but one night that cat got in the house. He said it might have scratched him to death, but he just got to the fireplace and got hold of the poker. When he stuck the poker in the fire to get it hot, that cat just disappeared. He said it went right through the keyhole of the front door. His youngest boy took sick and couldn't eat anything that he could hold on his stomach. They got the doctor to come, but he didn't do him any good at all. Lafe knew that it was the spell that the old witch woman had put on the boy.

Well, there was an old man, Jake Dobbins, who was known as a witch doctor. He knew how to take the witch's spell off. Lafe finally had him come in to see what he could do to help the boy. Old Mr. Dobbins—everyone called him "Uncle Jake"—came, and when he looked at the boy, he said he was pretty sure he knew what was wrong with him. Then he went out and brought in some small branches from a witch-hazel bush. He stripped the leaves off the limbs and put them in the bed all around the boy. He put the limbs in the fireplace and started a fire with them. Then he took a big piece of paper, and with some of the soot from the fireplace he drew a picture of the old witch, with her name printed on it. Then he burned that paper in the fire that he'd made with the witch-hazel branches. While the paper was burning, he kept murmuring some strange words. When the fire had all burned out, Uncle Jake said to Lafe, "Now I think your boy will be all right."

And the very next day that boy was out of that bed, and he

didn't get sick any more. But they didn't see the old witch woman for a long time, and some folks said that she had taken a pretty bad sick spell.

Well this old woman got to be up in her eighties, when she just disappeared. She was livin by herself at the time, and when folks didn't see her for some time, they went there to see about her. They couldn't find any sign of her anywhere. They went out to the woods and looked, for sometimes she had gone sangin' out in the woods, but she was never found. Some said they believed her time had come for the devil to take her away, for she had made an agreement with him to be a witch and he could take her. It's an awful thought, but its a true story.

HOW WITCHES GOT MILK AND BUTTER

Most of the witches of whom I have been told were women who lived alone, who had little means of support. Although they had no cows to supply milk and butter, the fact that they often had plenty of milk aroused the suspicions of neighbors. When one of the neighbors' cows would go dry, the old witch was immediately suspected of having taken the milk from the cow. The following group of tales tell how the witch got her milk.

This story, which I heard from Mrs. Lily Peters, of Nicholas County, was told to her by her great-grandfather when she was a child.

There was a family of Schoonovers who lived at Mud Lick. Mrs. Schoonover had several children, but her husband was dead. They didn't have any cows or hogs, and they put out only a small garden, but the children always looked very healthy. One evening the children came to the home of Mr. Thomas Floyd, just as the Floyds were getting ready to milk the cows. One of the girls said, "Mother doesn't have to milk cows to get milk." Mr. Floyd asked the girl how her mother could get milk if she didn't have any cows. The child replied, "Mother puts a dish-rag on a chair and milks, and we always have plenty of milk." When Mr. Floyd came back to the house after the milking, he said to his wife, "Now I know why our best cow quit giving milk."

THE MILK WITCH OF WOOD COUNTY

Millard Davis was ninety-two at the time he told this story. He lived on Winding Road in Wood County.

In the village where I was raised, there lived an old lady who was said to be a witch. She did strange things, but nobody ever said she actually hurt anyone. But any time she wanted milk, she would go out and spread a towel over a gooseberry bush. She'd let the ends dangle down, put the pail under it, and proceed to milk the pail full of milk. At milking time some of the neighbors' cows would go perfectly dry. I never saw her do this, but several others said they really saw her do it.

THE GILMER COUNTY WITCH PLAYS A TRICK

Lenore Danley, of Gilmer County, told this humorous story.

There was once an old woman who lived in the Sand Fork community of Gilmer County. Because she was so old and lived by herself, people suspected her of being able to do strange things, meaning that she was a witch. They said that she could stick a butcher knife in a tree or in a wall, hang a rag on it, and the milk would flow freely.

A young man went to her one day and asked her to teach him how to become a witch. She told him to go to an old abandoned cabin and stay there all night in the dark. She said a snake would come into the cabin, and he should speak to it and listen to what it said to him.

Well, he went there as she had told him, and about midnight here came a big black snake into the room. The boy got so scared that instead of speaking to the snake, he ran out of there as fast as he could run. The next morning they found that boy up on the top of the roof, calling for someone to help him down. They couldn't understand how in the world that boy got up there, for there was no ladder and the roof was so steep he had to straddle the ridge of the roof to keep from falling to the ground. The boy told them that when he ran out of that house, something lifted him up, just like a strong wind coming out of the ground, and the next thing he knew he was on top of the house. They all had a good laugh over it, and always after that they teased that boy nearly to death. He never let himself get close to that old woman after that.

THE BLACK CAT IS BEATEN

Many of the witch tales which have been told to me have already lived in oral tradition for many generations. John Russell, of Nicholas County, said his grandfather had told witch tales many times. The first one was about two old women who lived back in the mountains. They were both accused of being witches.

One day grandfather saw one of the women and made her angry about something. That night, just after he had gone to bed, he saw a black cat come in under the door. The cat went up to the fireplace, turned its back to the fireplace, and sat licking its paws. It sat there a little while, then came back and jumped on the bed and started choking him. He struggled with it, and finally got it by the front paws and beat it down over a chest that was by the bed. It finally got away from him and went out under the door. He swore at it as it disappeared, and he told it never to come back, and if it did he would get his gun and shoot it with a silver bullet that he had made.

The next day as he was going to work he met the old doctor. The doctor told my grandfather that he was going to see this old woman, because she had a bad fall and had almost broken her back. He was never troubled by the black cat any more.

ANOTHER WAY TO BREAK A SPELL

Mr. Russell then told me another one of his grandfather's witch tales.

One of grandfather's aunts lived near an old woman who was supposed to be a witch. His aunt was not afraid of the old woman, and would give her skimmed milk. One day the old woman said she wanted whole milk, but his aunt told her that she had to skim the cream off to make butter. The old woman got very angry and went away in a huff. The next day his aunt fixed the churning and started churning, but even after she had churned for an hour, there was no sign of butter. Well, she just knew that the old woman had put a spell on the cream so that no butter would come.

She put some cream in a skillet and put it on the fire. Then she took a small switch and beat the cream until it was all gone. After that she got plenty of butter when she churned. The old woman never did come back to get milk after that.

HOW TO KILL A WITCH

Andy Russell, who lived on a farm in Pocahontas County, West Virginia, said he didn't believe much in witches. He had worked hard all his life and had always got along pretty well with other people. He said, "I know there are strange things that go on, and I believe the old devil is still around tryin' to draw good folks away from the Lord." He continued:

My mother told me one time how when she was just a girl she had heard how a person could kill a witch. One was to make an image of the witch, using wax or some other soft material. The image didn't have to look exactly like the witch, but the witch's name had to be put on it. One had to take the image to the top of the highest mountain, and just as the sun rose over the mountain, the image had to be shot with a silver bullet from an old mountain rifle. The witch would then immediately develop bad trouble in the same part of her body where the image had been shot. Within three days the witch would be dead.

Now I never heard of anybody doing that, nor did my mother ever say that she knew of anybody doing it, but she said an old man had told her about it, and he had said that he could do it if anybody ever got in bad trouble with a witch.

WHITE BEAR

Willie Bone, who lived at Naoma, Raleigh County, West Virginia, said his mother used to tell the story of "White Bear." He said, "When we were small we used to gather around Mother like little chickens gathering around the mother hen, and she would tell us stories. The one we liked to hear her tell most was the story of the white bear." This story is not of American origin, but is one of the tales brought to this country

from old-world sources. A more elaborate version of this story
appears in Grandfather Tales, *edited by Richard Chase,*
Houghton Mifflin Company, 1948. Mr. Chase edited the story
from versions found in Virginia and North Carolina.
Here is the way Mr. Bone told the story:

There was a man lived way out in the country, who had
three daughters. Their names were Peggy, Meggy, and Nancy.
This man had to go several miles to get to the grocery store,
clean over the mountain, to buy groceries. So he got ready to
go to this grocery store over the mountain trail, and when he
got ready to leave, he asked the girls what kind of dresses they
wanted. Meggy said, "I'd like to have a dress as blue as the sky."
Well, he said, "Peggy, what kind of dress do you want?" "Well,
she said, "I'd like to have a yellow dress." He said, "Nancy, what
kind of dress do you want?" "Oh," she said, "Father, I don't
want any dress at all. All I want is for you to stop at the rose
patch as you come back and pick me a basket of roses."

So he went to the store and did his shopping at the store, and
on his way back he stopped at the rose patch and started picking
roses. There was a white bear in that rose patch. He came out
of there and asked the old man what he was picking those roses
for. He said he was picking them for his daughters. The bear
asked about the daughters, and asked what their names were.
The man said, "Their names are Peggy, Meggy, and Nancy." He
said he picked some roses for Peggy, and some for Meggy, and
he had picked just one for Nancy. The bear said, "Well, you pick
one and I'll pick two for Nancy. And I'll be there at your home
next Sunday morning, yes, I'll be there for Nancy."

Well, they thought the white bear would come, so they fixed
something like a hammock up in the corner of the house, and
they put Nancy up in there. Dreckly they saw the white bear
comin' a-ridin'. It turned out that he'd been put under a spell
by a witch, so that he could be a man of a day and a bear of a
night, or he could be a bear of a day and a man of a night. When
the witch put the spell on him she put a spot of blood on the

back of his shirt, and said that blood would stay there as long as the spell lasted, but if ever the blood could be washed out, the spell would come off.

He said to them, "Where's Nancy?" And they told him, "Nancy's not here, she's gone away." And he said, "No, she's not gone." And he took a knife and cut her down from that hammock.

Then he took Nancy away. He was riding one horse and leading another, so he put Nancy on the horse he was leading. He took her away and kept her for two years. After two years he brought her back home, and they had a baby with them. Now this white bear had accumulated a lot of money, and he had three stores and lots of wealth. So Nancy introduced him to the folks at home when they came in. His name was Barry Warren. So they talked there a while, and he got ready to leave. They thought that's all there was to it. But he took Nancy right along.

They stayed away three more years and came back again. This time they had another baby with them—there were two babies. They had a right smart of trouble over Nancy coming home that time, and she wouldn't go back with Barry Warren that time. So he started off up the mountain and went out of sight. Well, she started off after him, and she had those two children.

She went as far as she could, and she came to some women a-washing beside the creek. She asked them if they would keep one of the babies for her. She asked them if they had seen a strange man. They said, "Yes, there was a man passed here about two hours ago. And he told us women who were washing, that whichever one of us could wash the blood out of his shirt, why, he'd marry her." And they said that they'd both washed, and washed, and washed, but couldn't get the blood out.

So she went on, and she came to some more women a-washing, down by the river, and she asked them to take care of the other baby for her. She knew she was gaining ground on Barry Warren. So they told her that they'd keep the baby for her.

They said there was a man passed through here a while ago, and he said if either one of us women could wash the blood out of his shirt, he would marry her. So Nancy said to them, "Give me the shirt." They gave her the shirt, and she went to washin' on the old washboard, you know, and she just washed that blood out right now.

Well, she went on, and when it began to get dark, she called at a place and asked if they could keep her for the night. Well, they said they didn't know whether they could keep her or not, for a man had come to stay all night, and they had just one bed. Well, Nancy told them she would like to see that stranger. And they let her go into the room where he was. He turned his back to her. He'd heard her talking and knew her voice, and he turned his back to her. She pulled the blankets back and said to him, "You turn over here, Barry Warren, and speak to me." So he turned over and spoke to her, and she told him she'd come after him, and told him where the babies were, and she wanted him to take her and go on back home with her. He decided he'd do that.

They went back to where they collected the second child, and they went on then to where she'd left the first one. They came on back home then, and he didn't have to be a bear any longer, because when Nancy had washed the blood out of his shirt, the witch's spell was broken and he could be a man all the time now. So Barry Warren and his wife Nancy didn't have any more trouble.

A YOUNG MAN FIXES
THE WITCH OF BULL RUN

This story was contributed by Lenore Danley of Glenville, who said an old man living on Little Bull Run of Gilmer County told it to her. He told her the exact names of the persons concerned, and said every word of the story was true.

An old woman in the neighborhood had 'witched a young man living in the same neighborhood. He was annoyed very much at every kind of work he tried to do. If he tried to cut corn, he lost his corn cutter before he got to the field, or the stalks of the corn would not be there when he reached for them. Sometimes he could hear voices near him and hideous laughter, but he could not discern the words or the voices. If he called any of the livestock, it would run away from him. There just didn't seem to be anything he could do.

Things got so bad that he finally went into the woods at midnight in the light of the moon, where he found a long, slim young hickory. He named the hickory the name of the old woman who had 'witched him. Then he split that hickory where it stood and twisted it till it could not get loose. Then he returned home, and after that he had no more trouble. That old woman took to her bed and didn't leave the house for a long time. When people next saw her she was bent over. She told people she had got arthritis, but it was that twisted hickory that really fixed her.

RECOLLECTIONS OF WITCHCRAFT

When I was a young boy there was an old woman who lived not far from my boyhood home in Gilmer County, whom many people suspected of being a witch. Rumors got around that she could do strange things, and many of the young boys and girls became afraid of her. I had been warned by some of my playmates that I must never let this old woman look me in the eyes, for if she did, she could put a spell on me.

I am telling this incident from my own experience to illustrate how the belief in witchcraft probably accounted for much illness from fear and worry.

One day I was riding a horse, and rode up to a farmhouse to carry a message to the farmer from my grandfather.

Being too small to put my foot in the stirrup and dismount in the proper manner, I jumped down to the ground from the horse's back. When my feet hit the ground, I fell to my knees and raised my head so that I was looking toward the porch. There on the porch sat this old woman, staring at me. Her eyes seemed to be staring straight into my eyes.

My first fear was that this old woman had put a spell on me. When I got back home I was afraid to tell anyone about my experience. I became ill from worry and fear, wondering what effect the spell would have on me. After several days of worry, which made me almost ill, I told my mother what had happened and of my fear of being bewitched by the old woman. My mother, who didn't believe in witchcraft, soon dispelled my fears, and I was immediately well in mind and body.

I was at my grandmother's house one day, when one of my great-aunts came by on her way to the store. She stopped and was talking to my grandmother, when suddenly one of my grandmother's hens crowed like a rooster. My great-aunt said to my grandmother, "I tell you, there are strange things going on around here. That old woman has been busy again. You must kill that hen and burn it, or something terrible will happen." I do not remember what my grandmother did about the crowing hen, but I am sure that if she killed it, one of the visiting preachers had a good chicken dinner.

Once our closest neighbors, who lived about a quarter of a mile from us, discovered their hogs running around in circles until they were exhausted. It seemed that they would surely die if they did not stop this incessant running. The father of the family tried to get the hogs to eat corn, but they would not even stop long enough to drink the buttermilk in their trough. They had never seen hogs act like this, and they were pretty sure that the old witch woman had put a spell on them.

The father got a piece of white paper and drew a picture of the old woman. He said it didn't matter if the picture didn't look just like the old witch, just so he put her name on it. Then he burned the picture in the fireplace, and the very minute the paper burned to ashes, the hogs calmed down and ate all their feed. They had no more trouble after that.

There were many stories about the strange things that this old woman did. She put a spell on the cows of one family, so that no butter could be churned from the cream. The mother of the family, who was convinced that the old witch woman had put a spell on their cows, heated a poker until it was red-hot, then plunged it into the churn. It wasn't long until she got more butter from that one churning than she had ever got at one time.

Another family in the community had a cow that started giving bloody milk. They were pretty sure that the old witch woman had put a spell on that cow. They remembered that the old woman had come to their house and borrowed a pair of sheep shears, but had not returned them. They wondered what she wanted to do with sheep shears, for she didn't own any sheep. They supposed that she wanted to shear her big shepherd dog. Now they suspected that she had used the shears to put a spell on the cow.

Fortunately they knew what to do to break this spell. First, they found a large flat rock and laid it on the cow's back just over her hind legs. Then they cut three witch hazel switches and whipped the cow with them. The next morning the cow gave pure white milk. They warned the old woman that if she ever did anything like that again, they would know how to deal with her.

Appendix

❖❖❖❖❖❖❖❖❖❖

A CLASSIFICATION INDEX
OF WITCHES, GHOSTS AND SIGNS

Judy P. Byers[1]

Wayland Hand's system of classifying customary practices, folk cures, nature lore, and superstitions is employed here to supplement Patrick W. Gainer's work in *Witches, Ghosts and Signs*. The late Wayland D. Hand, professor at UCLA from 1937–1974, originally assembled a master file of American superstitions taken from many archives and virtually all published collections of folkloristic materials to aid in his editing The Frank C. Brown Collection of North Carolina Folklore, a project that occupied him from 1944 to 1964. Hand further refined his classification system to organize an encyclopedia of American popular beliefs and superstitions, but he died in 1986 before realizing that goal. The system he devised, however, remains invaluable to readers and researchers to facilitate finding analogues across cultural, temporal, and geographic barriers. Hand's system contains fourteen major categories, grouped under four broad headings: the cycle of

[1] The classifying and motifing of Gainer's *Witches, Ghosts and Signs* was accomplished with help by the students in my spring and fall 2006 Folk Literature courses at Fairmont State University, Fairmont, West Virginia, English 3387 and Folklore 3300: Lana Boyce, Terri Boyce, Macole Bunner, Jeremy Casto, Hannah Clutter, Michael DeVito, Sondra Edwards, Megan K. Haugh, Michael Hayes, Josie Henderson, Kristin Higginbotham, Kristin Knicely, Dominique Lacaria, Vanessa Lanham, Nancy Lilly, Brandon Manchion, Jennifer O'Connor, Nicole Reynold, Michelle Robertson, Meagan Rowan, Sara Sapp, Dana Sayre, Chris Skoloski, Allison Sypolt, Addie Wilson; Mark Carl's work culminated in a Senior Folklore Studies Project 2006, and Susan Long's work contributed to her M Ed with a folklore emphasis, 2007. A special thank you is extended to Cathy Calkins, graduate student assistant, The Frank & Jane Gabor WV Folklife Center, FSU.

human life, the supernatural, cosmology and the natural world, and miscellaneous superstitions. Many of the superstitions related to the first category of the human life cycle display concepts and habits of reasoning that can be traced to common practices in primitive cultures which have survived into modern times.[2]

THE WAYLAND HAND
CLASSIFICATION OF SUPERSTITIONS

A. *Related to the human life cycle*
1. Birth, infancy, childhood
2. Human body (folk medicine, healing)
3. Home, domestic pursuits
4. Economics, social relations
5. Travel, communication
6. Love, courtship, marriage
7. Death and funeral customs

B. *Supernatural*
8. Witchcraft, ghosts, magical practices
8a. Folk Religion[3]

C. *Superstitions about cosmology and the natural world*
9. Cosmic phenomena: time, numbers, seasons, etc.
10. Weather
11. Animals, animal husbandry
12. Fishing and hunting
13. Plants, plant husbandry

D. *Miscellaneous*
14. Wishing, general good and bad luck, modern beliefs

In order to classify customary practices, such as the folk cures listed on pp. 109–111 of Gainer's *Witches, Ghosts and Signs*, one would go to part A

---

[2] Jan Brunvand, *The Study of American Folklore* (New York: W. W. Norton and Company, 1998), p. 382.
[3] Brunvand, *The Study of American Folklore*, p. 390. Hand's system does not recognize folk religions, thus, the supplementary number, 8a.

of the Hand system, superstitions related to the human life cycle, and find subsection 2: Human body (folk medicine). In this section are traditional cures for ailments. In fact, the less medical science knows about an ailment, such as hiccups, warts, rheumatism, or the common cold, the more likely that there is a folk remedy for it (Brunvand, p. 383). All the folk cures listed on pp. 109-111 may be classified under the Hand system as A2:"Related to the human life cycle—Human body (folk medicine, healing)."

When Gainer's descriptions of traditional activities and customs refer to a superstition, the superstition is annotated with a reference to the traditional activity, the page on which it is described, the line or lines in which the superstition is presented, and the Hand classification section and number. Nature lore and general superstitions may fall into more than one category of the Hand classification system. For example, the superstition found on p. 118, "The new of the moon is the time to kill trees by ringing them," would fall into categories C9, because it deals with cosmology (the new moon), and C13, because it also mentions the care of plants or plant husbandry.

TRADITIONAL ACTIVITIES AND CUSTOMS, pp. 19–34

The Corn Shuckin'
    p. 22, line 7: When any man found a red ear of corn, he had the privilege of kissing the girl of his choice. A6
Halloween
    p. 27, line 18:"Dumb Suppers" were set at which girls sat in silence at a table where a chair was left vacant for a lover to occupy. A6
Christmas
    p. 28, in the third full paragraph: When people met on Christmas day they greeted each other with the phrase "Christmas Gift," and the one who spoke the greeting first was supposed to have good luck.   D14

FOLK CURES, pp. 109–111

These are all classified as A2: Related to the human life cycle—the human body (folk medicine and healing).

NATURE LORE AND RULES
FOR FARMING, pp. 112–120

Most of this lore may be classified under the broad division C in the Hand system: "Superstitions about cosmology and the natural world," subsection 10: "weather." However, lore dealing with the nature of coming seasons or rules for planting or animal husbandry which deal with moon signs also falls into C11, or C13. If planting or animal husbandry rules include planting by the signs or the moon, they are included under C9 ("Cosmic phenomena: time, numbers, seasons"). For each page of Nature Lore and Rules for Farming in *Witches, Ghosts and Signs*, each item of lore is listed in order, with the Hand classification following.

Page 113

Turkeys dance before a rain   C10
Sweating rocks are a sign of rain   C10
When the pitcher of water sweats excessively, it is going to rain   C10
When salt melts, it will rain soon   C10
If wool "snurls up" when you spin, it is a sign of rain   C10
When insects fly low over water it is a sign of rain   C10
When the fish jump above water, it is a sign of rain   C10
If swallows fly low, it is a sign of rain   C10

Page 114

If a lamp flickers continually, there will be rain   C10
When the corn twists, rain is coming   C10
A rain crow (dove) calling is a sign of coming rain   C10
When the tree frogs call more than usual, rain is coming   C10
When the fish worms come close to the top of the ground, it is a sign of
    coming rain   C10
If a rooster crows after six in the evening, his head will be wet before
    morning   C10
If chickens pick their feathers after a rain, there will be another rain
    soon   C10

If the fog lifts early, there will be rain   C10

Cows at peaceful rest in the evening mean rain before morning   C10

If there is rain on Whitsunday, there will be rain for seven Sundays   C10

A ring around the moon with no stars inside the ring means rain   C10

When gnats swarm, rain and warmer weather will soon follow   C10

When flies bite you, it will rain soon   C10

When the flies try to come in the house, it is a sign of rain   C10

When the red birds call in the morning, it will rain before night   C10

If the sun sets behind a cloud on Wednesday, it will rain before
    Sunday   C10

If it rains when the sun is shining, it will rain the next day at the same
    time   C10

When the evening's red and the morning's gray, It's the sign of a bonny,
    bonny day; When the evening's gray and the morning's red, The ewe and
    the lamb will go wet to bed   C10

Rain before seven, clear before eleven   C10

Page 115

If the leaves of the trees turn up on Monday, it will rain before
    Wednesday   C10

When the leaves of the poplar or grape turn up, it is a sure sign of
    rain   C10

When black snakes come out, it is a sign of coming rain   C10

There will be as many snows the following winter as there are rains in
    August   C10

If the smoke draws down the chimney, a change in the weather is due   C10

When telephone wires ring, a change in weather may be expected
    C10

If the camphor bottle is clear, the weather will be pretty   C10

The sun always shines at some time on Friday and Saturday   C10

A rainbow indicates that the rain is over   C10

The nearer the changes of the moon are to midnight, the fairer the
    weather will be until the next change of the moon   C10

When the Indian can hang his shot pouch on the corners of the moon,
    there will be fine weather   C10

When the smoke from the chimney rises straight in the air, the
weather will be fair; when it spreads out over the roof, the weather
will be foul   C10

When the fog lifts late, it will be a fine day   C10

When cobwebs can be seen on the ground in the morning, it will be a
fine day   C10

When the leaves of the aspen do not quiver, there is a hard storm
approaching   C10

When the pigs run about with straws in their mouths, a storm is
coming   C10

When the geese wander on the hills and fly homeward squawking, there
will be a storm within twenty-four hours   C10

If the rooster continues to crow at short intervals in the daytime, there
will be a hard rain within twelve hours   C10

When distant noises are heard plainly in the morning, there will be rain
before night   C10

Lightning in the north is a sign of dry weather   C10

Page 116

When the hornets build their nests high above the ground, it is a sign of
a hard winter. If nests are low, it will be mild   C9, C10

If there is thunder in February, there will be snow in May   C10

A late Easter brings a late spring; an early Easter, an early spring   C9

It always clears off in time to milk in the evening   C10

The wind always blows hardest at five o'clock, but always dies down just
after sundown   C10

If March comes in like a lamb, it will go out like a lion; if it comes in like
a lion, it will go out like a lamb   C9

If the groundhog sees his shadow on the second of February, there will
be six more weeks of cold weather; if he does not see his shadow,
winter is broken   C9

If the craw crabs throw up a mound around their holes, it will be a dry
summer; if they do not throw up a mound around their holes, the
summer will be a wet one   C9

When the locust blooms are heavy, it will be a cool summer   C9

When the shells on the nuts are thick, it means a hard winter   C9

When the fur on the animals is unusually heavy, it means a hard winter
     C9

When the wooly worm is entirely black, it will be a hard winter;
     however, if one end of the worm is light, that part of the winter will
     be mild   C9

After you hear the first katydid, it will be six weeks until the first
     frost   C9

If the excrement within the bowels of a butchered hog is thin, the winter
     will be mild; if it is thick, the winter will be cold   C9

When the squirrels put away many nuts, the winter will be severe   C9

Thunder in winter is a sign of colder weather   C10

As deep as the ground dries out in the summer, so will the freezing be
     the next winter   C9, C10

Thin corn husks mean a light winter; thick ones a heavy winter   C9

A cold winter follows a hot summer   C9

If the birds nest low, the river rises will be low that summer; if high, the
     rises will be high   C9

Page 117

Thunder will cause milk to sour   C10

If your hair curls, expect rain   C10

Plant beets when the sign is in the heart   C9, C13

To have good beets, let a growing person sow the seeds   C13

If you want tobacco to cure well, cut it in the new of the moon   C9,
     C13

Plant cabbage and tomatoes in alternate hills, and the tomatoes will
     never blight   C13

To hoe beans, tomatoes, or potatoes when the dew is on will cause them
     to blight   C13

Plant cabbage seeds while the sign is in the head   C9, C13

Sow early cabbage seeds on St. Patrick's Day   C13.

Plant late cucumbers when the sign is in the twins   C9, C13

Plant potatoes on Good Friday   C13

Sow flax seed on Good Friday   C13

What grows above the ground should be planted in the new of the
  moon; below, in the old of the moon   C9, C13
Plant corn when the sign is in the scale, and the ears will be heavy
  C9, C13
Plant corn when the white-oak leaves are the size of squirrel's ears
  C13
Plant corn when the dogwood is in full bloom   C13
Kill the first snake that you see in the spring, and no snake will bite
  you   C11
Always put wooden shingles on a house in the dark of the moon, or the
  shingles will turn up   C9
To keep a dog home, pull three hairs from the tip of his tail and put
  them under the doorstep   C11
Make all pickle stuff in the light of the moon, and the brine will rise
  quickly to cover it   C9
To make soap, stir it with a sassafras stick in the old of the moon   C9
Kraut or pickle beans will not keep if made by a woman during her
  menstrual period   C13
Beans planted in the new of the moon will climb up the corn, but if
  planted in the old of the moon, they will not climb   C9, C13

Page 118
  Plant corn in the dark of the moon so the ears will be low and
    heavy   C9, C13
  A heavy dogwood bloom means a good corn crop   C13
  Plant potatoes with the cut-side down for a good crop   C13
  When the lilac bloom is heavy, there will be a good corn crop   C13
  To ripen cider, set the barrel in the sun and place a black bottle in the
    bunghole   C13
  Briers should be cut in August when the sign is in the heart   C9, C13
  To cut brush so that it will not grow again, cut it on Ember Days   C13
  The new of the moon is the time to kill trees by ringing them   C9, C13
  Never peel the bark of a tree in the old of the moon   C9, C13
  Fruit is never killed by frost in the light of the moon   C9, C13
  There will be no fruit when apple blossoms do not fall under the tree   C13

Pick apples in the dark of the moon, and the bruised places will dry up; in the light of the moon, they will rot   C9, C13

Cut a limb off an apple tree in the light of the moon, and the stub will bark over; in the dark of the moon, and it will rot   C9, C13

When you plant peach seeds, name them after women who have borne many children, and the trees will be fruitful   C13

If hawks get the chickens, pick up a flat rock from the creek bed, place it in the bottom of the grate, and the hawks will leave   C11

To break a setting hen, tie a red ribbon around her neck, with the bow across her breast   C11

Keep a goat in the barn, and there will be no sick animals there   C11

No matter what time of the day you kill a snake, its tail will wiggle until sunset

Blacksnakes will suck cows   C11

Kill a snake that has sucked a cow, and the cow will go dry   C11

When a turtle bites, it will hold on until sunset   C11

A horsehair put in water will turn into a snake   C11

A toad will give you warts if you handle it   C11

If you plant climbing beans when the corner of the moon is down, the beans will crawl on the ground instead of climbing the pole   C9, C13

Page 119

It is good to set an odd number of eggs   C11

Put your hand in the nest of a turkey, and it will not lay more eggs there   C11

Thunder kills chickens just about to hatch   C10, C11

Butter will come easily all year when you do not mix the milk of April with the milk of May   A3

When you move a cat, grease its feet so that it will not go back   C11

When you move a cat, carry it backwards and it will not return   C11

The time to alter animals is when the sign is between the knee and the ankle   C9, C11

When a calf is weaned in the light of the moon, the cow will not bawl   C9, C11

If you kill a toad, the cows will give bloody milk   C11

If you milk a cow on the ground, she will go dry   C11

Pork killed in the old of the moon will shrink in the skillet   C9, C11

Pork killed in the light of the moon will turn to grease   C9, C11

Singe the hair of a rat and turn it loose, and all the other rats will follow it   C11

If you count your bee gums, all your bees will die   C11

When bees swarm, ring a bell or pound on tin cans to cause them to settle   C11

Hold your breath, and bees cannot sting you   C11

If a horse balks at night, he sees a ghost   C11, B8

If you see a white horse, the next woman you see will have red hair   B8

A horse with big ears has a good disposition   C11

A white mule will never die   C11

When a foal is dropped, measure the distance from the hoof to the shoulder point. Twice this distance will be the height of the horse when it is grown   C11

Cut a fish worm into pieces, and each piece will make a new worm   C11

Page 120

When two people hit their hoes together when working, they will be working together the next year   A4

When lightning strikes twice in the same place, there is mineral in the ground   C10

Sow grass seed in the light of the moon   C9, C13

Sow wheat in the old of the moon so that the ground will sponge it it up   C9, C13

Plant flowers when the sign is in the sign of the flowers   C9, C13

Set out onions in the old of the moon, and they will grow down in the light of the moon, and they will grow out of the ground   C9, C13

Plant radishes in the old of the moon   C9, C13

Peppers will grow better when planted by a red-headed woman   C13

Sow turnips between sundown and dark, and you will never fail of a crop   C13

When there is much honeydew, the bees will not winter well   C11

Where greenbriers grow, the land is too poor to sprout black-eyed
   peas   C13
Look under white walnuts for ginseng   C13
The number of rows on an ear of corn is always even   C13
Frost will never kill peaches that bloom in the dark of the moon   C9, C13

SUPERSTITIONS, PP. 121–134

The superstitions in this section fall in part A of Hand's classification system, which deals with the cycle of human life (A1 – A7), and in
part D, miscellaneous superstitions about wishing, general good and bad
luck, modern beliefs (D14). Superstitions which are associated with birth,
infancy, and childhood (A1) frequently deal with activities which would
predetermine the child's habits or nature.[4] Superstitions associated with
home and domestic pursuits (A3) usually concern cooking, clothing, and
housekeeping activities. These include the taboo against seating thirteen
at table, or leaving the house through the same door with which one has
entered. Superstitions associated with economic and social relations (A4)
concern habits relating to economic pursuits and one's interactions with
other people. Superstitions of games and sports fall into this category.[5] Travel and communications superstitions (A5) often mention good
days or times for embarking on a trip, signs of future trips, or visitors.
Superstitions about mail, telegrams, and telephones fit into this category
too.[6] Superstitions concerning love, courtship, and marriage (A6) specify
charms, divinations and practices to foretell or ensure a happy marriage.
Superstitions focused on death and funereal customs (A7) reflect our fear
of death and include not only signs and omens of a coming death, but traditional practices surrounding a death.[7] The last of Hand's categories ap-
plicable to this collection (D14) is a miscellaneous category and includes
general superstitions about good and bad luck.[8]

---

[4] Brunvand, *The Study of American Folklore*, p. 382.
[5] Brunvand, *The Study of American Folklore*, p. 385.
[6] Brunvand, *The Study of American Folklore*, p. 386.
[7] Brunvand, *The Study of American Folklore*, p. 387.
[8] Brunvand, *The Study of American Folklore*, p. 394.

Page 123

It is bad luck to kill a cricket   D14

If someone gives you flowers for planting and you thank them for the flowers, the flowers will die   C13

You should always leave a house by the same door you enter, or you will have bad luck   D14

If a picture is tilting on the wall, it means bad luck   D14

It will bring good luck if on New Year's Day you cook cabbage and black-eyed peas together and put a dime in them   D14

If the birds get the combings from your hair, they will make a nest of it, and you will always have a headache   A2

If on New Year's Day a male enters your house first, it means good luck; if a female enters first, it means bad luck   D14

If you are touched by a broom while someone is sweeping, it means bad luck   D14

If you sweep a circle around a boy or girl, he or she will never marry   A6

If you drop a spoon, a female guest is coming   A5

If you drop a fork, a male guest is coming   A5

If you wear a penny in your shoe, it will bring good luck   D14

It is good luck to find a penny   D14

It is good luck to find a button, if you keep it   D14

If it rains on your wedding day, it is a sign that you will shed many tears during your married life   A6

When you are moving, it is bad luck to move parsley roots   D14

It is bad luck to accept parsley roots from anyone   D14

It is bad luck to find an open safety pin   D14

To have good luck, always get out of bed on the right side   D14

Put your right shoe on first to have good luck   D14

It is bad luck to bring a hoe in the house   D14

If you kill a toad, your cow will give bloody milk   D14

It is bad luck to raise an umbrella in the house   D14

If you spill salt, you must throw some salt over your left shoulder to avoid bad luck   D14

It is bad luck to rock a rocking chair with no one in it   D14

A howling dog means death   A7

Page 124

If four stalks of a lily come up to bloom, someone in the family will die
that year   A7

If a person cuts out a window of his house and makes a door, someone in
the family will die that year   A7

If anyone eats fruit that has grown in a graveyard, he will die before the
year is out   A7

It is bad luck to step on the cracks in a sidewalk   D14

If a woman cuts out a dress for herself on Friday and does not finish it
on the same day, she will die before the year is out   A7

It is bad luck to carry an axe in the house   D14

The dead must always be buried to face the rising sun   A7

A storm follows the death of old people. Nature is mourning   A7

If the walls creak, it means a death soon   A7

It is bad luck to watch some one out of sight   D14

If the thread knots while one is sewing, it means the one who is sewing
will die   A7

It is bad luck to tell some one good-bye   D14

It is bad luck to find a five-leaf clover   D14

It is good luck to find a four-leaf clover   D14

It is bad luck for three persons to use the same match to light their
cigarettes   D14

Three lighted lamps on one table means bad luck is coming   D14

If you drop a dish rag, someone who is hungry is coming   A5

When the hands on the clock are straight up and down, put a cake in the
oven and it will always come out well   A3

If someone jumps over you, your growth will stop   A2

If you eat pie on Tuesday, you will become ill   A2

If you eat fish and drink milk at the same time, you will be poisoned   A2

If you step over a broom, you will never be married   A6

If a bird flies in the window, someone in the family will die   A7

If a picture is broken in the home, the one in the picture will die   A7

If you receive a knife as a gift, you must give the donor a penny to
prevent a broken friendship   A4

If your right hand itches, you will receive money   A4

Page 125

If your left hand itches, you will shake hands with a stranger   A4

If you break a mirror, you will have bad luck for seven years   D14

If a baby looks into a mirror before it is a year old, it will not live to
maturity   A1

It is bad luck to sweep the floor after the sun goes down   D14

It is bad luck for a black cat to cross the path in front of you   D14

It is bad luck to pass people on the stairways   D14

It is bad luck for a hen to crow   D14

It is bad luck for a girl to whistle   D14

If a child's fingernails are cut before it is a year old, it will be a thief   A1

If you sing before breakfast, you will cry before supper   A4

It is bad luck to sell a hive of bees   D14

The hooting of an owl close to the house means bad luck   D14

Playing with a comb will cause a child to stammer   A1

When two persons are walking, it is a sign they will quarrel if they walk
on different sides of a tree or other object   A4

The bad luck will be averted if they say, "Bread and butter"   D14

When you buy a horse, it is good luck to change his name   D14

If you cannot find a lost article, spit in the palm of your hand; while
saying, "Spitter, Spitter, spider, tell me where that (name of the article)
is and I'll give you a drink of cider," hit the spittle with your right
forefinger. Follow the direction where most of the spittle goes, and you
will find the article   A3

If you look at the moon through a knothole, you will never be married   A6

If two forks are at a place-setting on the table, the one who sits there will
get married   A6

If there is a feather crown in your pillow, it is a sign that you are going to
heaven when you die   B8

When you pull a tooth, drive it in an apple tree, and good luck will
follow   D14

Lightning-struck wood burned in the cooking stove will cause the house
to be struck by lightning   C10

If you carry a rabbit's foot in your pocket, you will have good luck   D14

Page 126

If you breathe on a bird's egg, the ants will eat it   C11

Hide a tooth under a rock and go back later, and you will find money   A4

If you take the last piece of anything, you will be an old maid unless you kiss the cook   A6

If a corpse is very cold, there will not be another death in the house for that year   A7

The man of the house must set out the rambler rose if it is to live   C13

When you find a hair pin, press it together. If the ends are even, you will meet a boy; if uneven, you will meet a girl   A4

If you eat from an uneven plate, you will have bad luck   D14

If you shorten a baby's dress in May, you are shortening its days   A1

It is good luck to take a dog with you when you move, but bad luck to take a cat   D14

When a horseshoe is hung with the open end up, your luck will not run out   D14

A rabbit crossing your path will bring good luck   D14

To meet a cross-eyed person is a sign of good luck   D14

To lay your hand on the hump of a hunchback person is the best of luck   D14

This rhyme should be kept in mind while out walking:

See a pin and pick it up,

And all the day you'll have good luck;

See a pin and let it lie,

Bad luck to you will fly   D14

It is a sign of good luck to open the Bible at random and find the words "verily, verily" on the page   D14

When you get a small hen's egg, throw it over the house to avoid bad luck   D14

When you find a five-leaf clover, you can give the bad luck away by giving it to another person, and he will have good luck   D14

To count the teeth in a comb brings bad luck   D14

It is bad luck to drop a comb, but put your foot on the comb that has been dropped and your luck will turn   D14

Page 127

When you return to the house for something that has been forgotten, sit down in a chair before leaving again to avoid bad luck   D14

When you shake hands two times in saying goodby, do it again to avoid bad luck   D14

Thirteen people at the table brings bad luck   D14

Passing under a ladder brings bad luck   D14

Looking at the new moon through trees brings bad luck   D14

When playing cards it is bad luck to pick up the cards one at a time as they are being dealt   D14

It brings bad luck to play cards across the grain of the table   D14

It is bad luck to sit in a rocking chair to play cards   D14

For a lamp chimney to break in the hand without apparent cause is a sign of bad luck   D14

It is bad luck to change a baby's name   D14

It is bad luck to close an open gate   D14

To turn a coffin in the house will bring bad luck   D14

It is bad luck to postpone a wedding   D14

It is bad luck to carry a fishing pole into the house   D14

When hunting, it is bad luck to cross a different part of the fence from the person in front of you   D14

It is unlucky to throw a gift away   D14

To break something on New Year's day will bring bad luck for the rest of the year   D14

It is unlucky to marry a person born in the same month   D14

It is bad luck to spill ink   D14

To wash the palm of a baby's hand will wash his luck away   D14

It is bad luck for two persons to make a bed   D14

It is bad luck to burn bread   D14

It is bad luck to count the box cars in a train   D14

It is bad luck to count the carriages in a funeral procession   D14

If sassafras is burned in the fireplace, bad luck will follow   D14

To shake the table cloth after sundown brings bad luck   D14

To climb out a window and not climb back will bring bad luck   D14

Page 128

If you sneeze while putting on your shoes, you must go back to bed to
    avoid bad luck   D14

To lean a broom against the bed will bring bad luck   D14

To sit with crossed feet in a rocking chair will bring bad luck   D14

To dream of gathering eggs is a sign of bad luck   D14

To move into a house before the fire which has been made by the former
    dwellers burns out, brings bad luck   D14

You can turn aside the bad luck when a black cat crosses your path by
    spitting on its tracks   D14

It is bad luck for a piece of bread to fall with the buttered side up   D14

If a clock stops without being run down, a dear friend will die at the
    hour at which the clock stopped   A7

If you hear three knocks at the door, someone in your family will
    die   A7

A falling star is a sign of death   A7

If a bat flies into the room, it is a sign of death   A7

When a cedar tree that has been set out has limbs long enough to cover
    the coffin of the person who set it out, he will die   A7

After a funeral, whichever sex leaves the graveyard first will be the next
    to be buried there   A7

If a filled grave sinks quickly, there will be another death in the family
    soon   A7

Hang your hat on a doorknob, and you are making the sign of a death in
    the family   A7

If a board warps in the porch, it is a sign of a death in the family   A7

If a peach tree blooms twice in the year, it is a sign of death in the
    family   A7

If an apple tree with blossom on it falls, it means a death   A7

It is bad luck to lend money in a card game   D14

To change bad luck while playing cards, put on your hat   D14

To change bad luck while playing cards, exchange seats with another
    player   D14

To sit in a card game with a cross-eyed man will bring bad luck   D14

Page 129

It is bad luck to start a journey on Friday   D14

Friday is an unlucky day to start anything you cannot complete   D14

To polish your shoes on your feet brings bad luck   D14

When you stumble over an object, go back and walk over it without stumbling to avoid bad luck   D14

It is bad luck for a whip-poor-will to light on the roof of a house   D14

To kill a spider brings bad luck   D14

For a picture to drop out of the frame means bad luck   D14

It is bad luck to cut the fingernails on Thursday   D14

It is bad luck for an animal to die in one's hand   D14

It is bad luck to boast of immunity from sickness, but the bad luck can be avoided by knocking on wood   D14

It is bad luck to count the buttons on another's clothes   D14

It is bad luck to visit a graveyard after dark   D14

It is bad luck to step or walk over a grave   D14

It is bad luck to meet a hearse   D14

It is bad luck for the head of the family to drown a cat   D14

To mend a garment you are wearing brings bad luck   D14

It is bad luck to change a garment that you have put on wrong side out   D14

A winding sheet, made when the melted wax clings around the candle and hardens, is sign of death in the family   A7

If a woman tears her wedding shoes, she will be beaten by her husband   A6

If a pillow falls off the wedding bed, the one who lies on it first will die first   A7

Whoever sleeps first on the wedding night will die first   A7

As long as you keep some of the bread of your first wedded meal, you will never be in want   A6

If a bride breaks her wedding ring, she will be a widow soon   A6

If a wedding ring be lost, the couple will separate   A6

To awaken the bride on her wedding morning is bad luck. Let her sleep as long as she will   A6

Page 130

For a bride to put her bare feet on the floor on the night of the wedding
is unlucky   A6

If a bride puts on her left shoe first, her married life will be unhappy   A6

If you go into a vacant house, throw a ball of yarn and say, "I pull, who
winds?" The one you are to marry will answer you   A6

Put the letters of the alphabet in a pan of water under your bed. The next
morning the initial of your future husband will be turned over   A6

When two people meet on the stairsteps, it is a sign of a wedding   A6

Walk backwards nine steps, and you will see a hair the color of the
person's hair you are to marry   A6

If anyone should see the bride's veil before the wedding, her married life
will be unhappy   A6

If the bridesmaid is older than the bride, she should wear something
green, or else she may never marry   A6

If a kettle of hot water is poured over the doorstep which the bride
crosses, there will be another wedding in that house within a year   A6

For good luck the bride must wear: Something old, something new, /
Something borrowed, something blue, / And a gold dollar in her shoe   A6

Two lovers will never agree after their marriage if both wipe their faces
on the same towel   A6

He who is needy when married, will be rich when buried   A6

If a boy and a girl meet by chance at a stile, they will be lovers   A6

Put three holly leaves under your pillow at night and name each leaf.
The one that is turned over in the morning will be the name of your
husband   A6

Put a four-leaf clover in the Bible. The man you meet while you are
carrying it will be your husband   A6

Hold the bride's dress on your lap for ten minutes, and you will be a
bride within the year   A6

Page 131

On the first day of May before sunrise, if you see a snail within a shell,
your future husband will have a house. If the snail is outside the shell,

he will have none. Sprinkle meal in front of the snail and it will form the initial of the man you are to marry   A6

Kiss a baby on the ninth day after its birth, and the next man you kiss will be your future husband   A6

Go fishing on the first day of May. A bite means a beau; a catch means you will get a husband within the year   A6

Put a pea pod with nine peas over the door. If a married man comes under it first, you will not be married within the year; if a single man, you will be married   A6

If you fall upstairs, you will not be married within the year   A6

Eat the point of a piece of pie first and you will be an old maid   A6

If your stocking comes down, you will be an old maid   A6

If you look under the bed, you will never marry   A6

If anyone sweeps around you, you will never marry   A6

When two young girls sleep together for the first time, if they tie their big toes together and the string is broken in the night, the one who has the shortest piece of string will marry first   A6

The white spots on your nails tell how many lovers you will have   A6

If you splash water on yourself while washing clothes, you will get a drunken husband   A6

If you cannot make a good fire, you will not get a good husband   A6

Here's a warning for the bride-to-be: Change your name and not the letter / Change for the worse and not the better   A6

If you go bare-footed, this rhyme may be useful: Stub your toe, kiss your thumb, / Kiss your beau before one   A6

Walk around a wheat field on the first day of May and you will meet your mate   A6

Put a slice of wedding cake under your pillow for seven nights, and the seventh night you will dream of your future husband   A6

Page 132

If a black cat takes up its home at a house, the unmarried daughters will have a good chance to marry   A6

If a bride wears another girl's garter when she is married, the girl will be married within the year   A6

The number of nails in the horseshoe which you pick up will be the number of years until you are married   A6

On Hallowe'en if you can eat an apple that is suspended on a string from the ceiling, you will marry within the year   A6

As many candles as are left on the birthcake after you blow once, that many years it will be till you are married   A6

On the first day of May, look in a well, and you will see the face of your future husband   A6

If you can blow the down from the dandelion in one blow, you will get the wish you make   D14

If two persons who think of the same thing at the same time hook their little fingers together and make a wish, the wish will come true   D14

If you see the new moon over your right shoulder and make a wish, the wish will come true   D14

When you find a four-leaf clover, swallow it and make a wish, and the wish will come true   D14

A wish made in a bed never before slept in will come true   D14

Sleep with the Bible under your head for three nights in a row, and you will dream of your future husband   A6

When you see the first star at night, say: Starlight, starbright, / First star I see tonight, / Wish I may, wish I might / Have the wish I wish tonight   D14

Make a wish while putting a ring on another person's finger, at the same time stating how long the ring is to stay on. If the ring is not removed during that time, the wish will come true   D14

When two persons pull the wishbone of the chicken, the one who gets the larger part gets the wish   D14

Page 133

Hang a wishbone over the front door, and the first man who passes under it is the man you will marry   A6

When you have put on a garment wrong side out, make a wish and it will come true   D14

Save the tip end of the pie, make a wish as you eat it, and the wish will come true   D14

When your dress skirt is turned up, spit on it and make a wish, and the
wish will come true   D14

If a pregnant woman passes her hands over her body, she will give the
baby a birthmark   A1

A woman in labor should hold salt between her hands   A1

Put sugar on the window to make the baby come   A1

If a baby loses its shoe, it will be rich   A1

Carry a new-born baby downstairs before it is carried upstairs so that it
will have success in life   A1

The number of wrinkles on your forehead indicate the number of
children you will have   A1

If a baby's fist does not close over money which is placed in its hand, it
will always be poor   A1

If the hand of a new-born baby be open, it will have a generous
disposition. If it is closed, it will be stingy   A1

If you see a man leading a horse with a side-saddle on Sunday, it is sure
that there will be a birth in that neighborhood within the week   A1

Your baby will resemble the person to whom you first carry it   A1

In time of war there will be more boys born than girls   A1

When a new-born child is veiled, it will have the gift of second sight   A1

If anyone steps over a baby, it will not grow for a year   A1

A child born on Christmas day can understand the speech of
animals   A1

You have a right to kiss a girl when she makes a face at you   A4

Kiss a girl when you find her under the mistletoe   A4

Kiss a girl when you find her under the wishbone of a chicken   A4

Pare an apple in a single long strip, throw the peeling over your left
shoulder, and it will form the initial of the first name of the person
whom you will marry   A6

Page 134

Burn the match to the end, and it will make the initial of the first name
of the man you are to marry   A6

When you hear the first robin sing in the spring, sit down on a rock and
take off your left stocking. If there is a hair in it, your sweetheart will
call on you soon   A6

If you take the last piece of bread off the plate when it is not offered, you
will never be married, but if you take it when it is offered, you will
marry well   A6

When your shoe is untied, someone is thinking of your love   A6

If your thumbs turn back at the end, you will be a good housekeeper   A3

Shut your fist over your thumb for good luck   D14

To cross your legs when playing cards will bring good luck   D14

Sleep on mustard seeds, and witches cannot bother you   B8

For good luck, eat pancakes on Shrove Tuesday   D14

If a horse is restless in the morning, witches have been riding it in the
night   B8

When a person sneezes, say "God bless you," and it will bring good
luck   D14

THE STITH THOMPSON
MOTIF-INDEX FOR FOLK-LITERATURE

The smallest transferable unit from one instance of a discourse
to another is called a "motif." The standard index of motifs was first produced by Stith Thompson at Indiana University between 1932–36 under
the title *Motif-Index of Folk-literature; A Classification of Narrative Elements
in Folk-tales, Ballads, Myths, Fables, Mediæval Romances, Exempla, Fabliaux,
Jest-books, and Local Legends*. Scholars and folklore practitioners have, since
then, augmented it with many examples of motifs not found in the original
set of motifs which he drew mostly from published sources, although his
six-volume work contained about 40,000 distinct motifs carefully categorized for ease of reference, and it has succeeded in providing the basic structure for folk-tale classifications throughout the English-speaking world.
Motifs involving animals in significant ways, for example, are categorized
under (B); those that focus on social, religious or other taboos occur under
(C); ogres (including witches) are under (G); unnatural cruelty is listed
under (S); and matter involving sex is under (T). Thompson's *Motif-Index*

is a 6-volume guide to all the various motifs found in a variety of folk literatures, including myths, legends, tall tales, and other oral narratives, not just folk fairy tales.

After a general description of the elements of the motif, a letter is given as the first item in classifying the motif; this is followed by a number. Decimal points are used to break these classifications down into even smaller subunits. G265, for instance, is used to identify the motif, "Witch abuses property." In breaking down Gainer's tale, "Uncle Johnnie Bewitches the Cows" on pages 142–144, we find G265.8. "Witch bewitches objects" as part of the analysis which may be sub-categorized as "Witch bewitches household objects. G265.8.1."

Because the analysis of folk- and oral-literatures lends itself to so many applications, including literary, sociological, psychological, and historical, the ability to locate tales with the elements one wishes to examine closely is particularly helpful. Not only can one examine these tales in Thompson's *Motif-Index*, but the scholarship on folktales makes use of the system as well, and this opens up an ever-increasing catalog of comparative data.

GHOSTLORE, pp. 35–99

Jim Barton's Fiddle (pp. 37–44)
    Ghosts of objects   E530.
    Other ghostly objects   E539.
    Ghost plays musical instruments   E554.
    Mysterious ghostlike noises heard   E402.
    Invisible ghost plays musical instrument   E402.1.3.

The Ghost of Mrs Green (pp. 44–45)
    Return from dead to reveal murder   E231.
    Revenant as a woman   E425.1.

The Woman Who Came Crying (pp. 45–46)
    Ghost seen by two or more persons; they corroborate the
        appearance   E421.5.
    Revenant as a woman   E425.1.
    Fight of a revenant with a living person   E461.

Ghost cries and screams   E402.1.1.3.
Ghost sobs   E402.1.1.6.

The Passing Soul (pp. 46–47)
Soul leaves body at death   E722.
Forms of the soul as it leaves body   E722.1.
Soul as a black or white entity   E722.1.2.
Soul as light   E742.

The Ghost of the Jilted Girl (pp. 47–48)
Malevolent return from the dead   E200.
Dead lover's malevolent return   E210.
Dead sweetheart haunts faithless lover   E211.
Ghost pursues man   E261.4.
Ghost disturbs sleeping person   E279.2.
Ghost pulls bedclothing from sleeper   E279.3.
Ghost haunts buildings   E280.
Ghost haunts house   E281.
Footsteps of invisible ghost heard   E4202.1.2.
Miscellaneous sounds made by ghost of human being   E402.1.8
Ghost visible to one person alone   E421.1.1.
Fight of revenant with living person   E461.
Ghosts cannot cross rapid stream   E434.3.

The Vengeful Ghost of the Murdered Girl (pp. 48–50)
Ghost disturbs sleeping person   E279.2.
Miscellaneous sounds made by ghost of human being   E402.1.8
Fight of revenant with a living person   E461.
Mysterious ghostlike noises heard   E402.
Murdered person cannot rest in grave   E413.
Invisible ghost   E421.1.

The Ghost of the Peddler on Third Run (pp. 50–51)
Ghost rides in carriage, disappears suddenly at certain spot   E332.3.2.
Ghost haunts scene of former misfortune, crime, or tragedy   E334.
Ghost seen by two or more persons; they corroborate the
    appearance   E425.1.
Headless revenant   E422.1.1.

The Collins Betts Peddler (p. 51)
  Ineradicable blood stain after bloody tragedy   E422.1.11.5.1

The Crying Infant (pp. 51–52)
  Ghost laid by reburial   E441.
  Ghost cries and screams   E402.1.1.3.

The Headless Horseman of Powell Mountain (pp. 52–53)
  Murdered person cannot rest in grave   E413.
  Headless revenant   E422.1.1.
  Actions of headless revenant   E422.1.1.3.
  Headless ghost rides a horse   E422.1.1.3.1.
  Road-ghosts   E272.
  Non-malevolent road ghosts   E332.
  Ghost of murdered person haunts burial spot   E334.2.1.
  Invisible ghost jingles chain   E402.1.4.
  Sound made by ghostly object   E402.3.

The Shue Murder Case (pp.53–54)
  Ghost visible to one person alone   E421.1.1.
  Ghost disturbs sleeping person   E279.2.
  Ghost tells name of murderer   E231.1.
  The unquiet grave   E410.
  Murdered person cannot rest in grave   E413.
  Return from dead to reveal murder   E231.

The Tragic Story of Ellen and Edward (pp. 54–57)
  Spectral ghosts   E421.
  Ghost seen by two or more persons; they corroborate the
    appearance   E421.5
  Revenant in female dress   E422.4.4.
  Revenant as woman   E425.1.
  Ghost of tragic lover haunts scene of tragedy   E334.2.3.
  Ghost of suicide seen at death spot or nearby   E334.4.
  Vocal sounds of ghost of human being   E402.1.1.
  Ghost cries and screams   E402.1.1.3.
  Revenant as lady in white   E425.1.1.

The Lover's Ghost (pp. 57–58)
  Luminous ghosts   E421.3.
  Ghost seen by two or more persons; they corroborate the
    appearance   E421.5.
  Soul as black or white entity   E722.1.2.
  Ghost haunts burial spot   E334.2.
  Twining branches grow from graves of lovers   E631.0.1.

A Haunted House (pp.58–59)
  Mysterious ghostlike noises heard   E402.
  Sounds made by invisible ghosts of animals   E402.2.
  Ghost in white   E422.4.3.
  Revenant in female dress   E422.4.4.
  Revenant as swine   E423.1.5.
  Ghost of hog   E521.5.
  Revenant in human form   E425.
  Revenant as woman   E425.1.
  Revenant as lady in white   E425.3.
  Revenant as child   E425.3.
  Ghost cries and screams   E402.1.1.3.
  Ineradicable bloodstain from bloody tragedy   E422.1.11.5.1.

The Poltergeist of Petersburg (pp. 59–60)
  Ghost haunts house   E281.
  Ghost seen by two or more persons; they corroborate the
    appearance   E421.5.
  Ghost disturbs sleeping person   E279.2.
  Ghost pulls bedclothes from sleeper   E279.3.
  Ghost pulls off blanket from sleeper   E544.2.
  Return from the dead to reveal hidden treasure   E371.
  Ghost directs man to hidden treasure   E545.12.
  Treasure pointed out by supernatural creature   N538.
  The dead foretell the future   E545.17.
  Other actions of revenants   E599.
  Ghosts move furniture   E599.6.
  Poltergeist makes noises   F473.5.
  Miscellaneous actions of poltergeist   F473.6.

The Mother-in-Law's Revenge (pp. 60–61)
    Poltergeist makes noise   F473.5.
    Ghost haunts particular room in the house   E281.3.
    Miscellaneous acts of malevolent ghosts   E299.
    Crash as of breaking glass, though no glass is found broken   E402.1.6.

The Ghost Rider (pp. 62–63)
    Revenant with cold lips   E422.1.4.
    Return from dead to return and ask back love token   E311.
    Dead lover's friendly return   E310.
    Ghost rides on horseback with rider   E332.3.1.
    Ghost rides horse   E581.2.

The Ghost Rides with her Lover (pp. 64–65)
    Ghost rides on horseback with rider   E332.3.1.
    Ghost haunts burial spot   E334.2.
    Ghost rides horse   E581.2. (Similar to E332.3.2. in that the ghost
        disappears at the specific spot.)

The Dog Ghost of Peach Tree (p .65)
    Animal ghosts   E520.
    Ghost of domestic beast   E521.
    Ghost of dog   E521.2.
    Ghost seen by two or more people; they corroborate the
        appearance   E421.5.
    Features of ghostly dog   E423.1.1.2.
    Color of ghostly dog   E423.1.1.1.
    Revenant as dog   E423.1.1.

The Hitch-Hiker (pp. 66–67)
    The vanishing hitchhiker   E332.3.3.1.
    Ghost of person killed in accident seen at death or burial spot
        E334.2.2.
    Person meets ghost on the road   E332.2.
    Ghost on road asks traveler for a ride   E332.3.
    Ghost asks for ride in automobile   E332.3.3.

The Phantom Wagon (pp. 67–68)
 Ghostlike conveyance   E535.
 Phantom coach (wagon) and horses   E535.1.
 Ghostly wagon   E535.2.
 Murdered person cannot rest in grave   E413.
 Ghost reenacts scene from own lifetime   E337.
 Ghost rides in carriage, disappears suddenly at certain spot   E332.3.2.

Add's Image (pp. 68–69)
 Revenant as face or head   E422.1.11.2.
 Ghost walks through solid substance   E572.

The Graveyard Ghost (p.69)
 Revenant in human form   E425.
 Ghost haunts burial spot   E334.2.

The Peddler's Ghost of Maysville (pp. 70–71)
 Mysterious ghostlike noises heard   E402.

The Ghosts of Echo Rock (pp.71–76)
 Vocal sounds of ghosts of human beings   E402.1.1.
 Ghost sings   E402.1.1.4.

Three Headless Ghosts (pp. 76–77)
 Ghosts haunt buildings   E280.
 Ghost disturb sleeping persons   E279.2.
 Headless revenant   E422.1.1.
 Actions of headless revenant   E422.1.1.3.

The White Bird (p.77)
 Dead wife returns in form of a bird   E322.4.
 Appearance of ghost serves as a death omen   E574.
 Revenant as bird   E423.3.

The Ghost of the Murdered Storekeeper (pp. 78–79)
 Mysterious ghostlike noises heard   E402.
 Ghost disturbs sleeping person   E279.2.
 Ghost pulls bedclothes from sleep   E279.3.

Ghost pulls off blanket from sleeper   E544.2.
Ghost leaves no footprints   E421.2.1.
Ghosts haunt buildings   E280.
Ghost haunts house   E281.
Non-malevolent ghost haunts house   E338.

The Ghost of the Mistreated Husband (p. 79)

Ghosts haunt house   E281.
Mysterious ghostlike noises heard   E402.
Noises caused by ghosts of a person   E402.1.
Vocal sounds of ghost of human being   E402.1.1.
Ghost moans   E402.1.1.2.
Ghost cries and screams   E402.1.1.3.
Ghost slams door   E402.1.7.
Ghost disturbs sleeping person   E279.2.
Ghost pulls bedclothes from sleeper   E279.3.
Ghost pulls off blanket from sleeper   E544.2.
Revenant as a dog   E423.1.1.
Ghost in white   E422.4.3.
Revenant in human form   E425.

The Peddler's Ghost of Pendleton County (p. 80)

Invisible ghost jingles chains   E402.1.4.
Footsteps of invisible ghost heard   E402.1.2.
Mysterious ghostlike noises heard   E402.
Ineradicable bloodstain after bloody tragedy   E422.1.11.5.1.
Ghost laid when house it haunts is destroyed or changed   E451.8.

The Old Haunted House of Nicholas County (p. 81)

Mysterious ghostlike noises heard   E402.
Vocal sounds of ghost of a human being   E402.1.1.
Ghost moans   E402.1.1.2.
Ghost cries and screams   E402.1.1.3.
Ghosts haunt house   E281.
Ghost in white   E422.4.3.
Revenant in female dress   E422.4.4.
Revenant in human form   E425.

Revenant as child   E425.3.
Ghost of murdered child   E225.

A Mysterious Disappearance (pp.82–83)
Ineradicable bloodstain after bloody tragedy   E422.1.11.5.1.
Ghost cries and screams   E402.1.1.3.

The Fireside Ghost (p. 83)
Revenant as a child   E425.3.
Ghost seen by two or more persons; they corroborate the
    appearance   E421.5.
Dead without proper funeral rights cannot rest   E412.3.
Ghost laid by reburial   E441.

The Chain (p. 84)
Mysterious ghostlike noises are heard   E402.

The Haunted House at Renick (pp. 84–85)
Mysterious ghostlike noises heard   E402.
Ghost sings   E402.1.1.4.
Footsteps of invisible ghost heard   E402.1.2.
Person otherwise killed by accident cannot rest   E414.1

The Stroop House Ghost (pp. 85–86)
Mysterious ghostlike noises heard   E402.
Ghost moans   E402.1.1.2.

The Informing Revenant (pp. 86–87)
Return from dead to reveal murder   E231.
Ghost visible to one person alone   E421.1.1.
Dead announces own death   E545.3.
Ghost rides horse   E581.2.

A Ghost Returns for His Head (pp. 87–88)
Walking ghost laid   E440.
Headless revenant   E422.1.1.
Person with missing bodily member cannot rest   E419.7.
Ghost laid when its wishes are acceded to   E459.3.
Persons who die violent or accidental deaths cannot rest in grave   E411.10.

The Woman in White (p.88)

Persons who die violent or accidental deaths cannot rest in grave
E411.10.

Ghost seen by two or more persons; they corroborate the
appearance   E421.5.

Revenant as lady in white   E425.1.1.

Ghost in white   E422.4.3.

Revenant in female dress   E422.4.4.

The Headless Rider of Spruce Lick (pp. 88–89)

Headless revenant   E422.1.1.

Actions of headless revenant   E422.1.1.3.

Persons who die violent or accidental deaths cannot rest in grave
E411.10.

Murdered person cannot rest in grave   E413.

Person with missing bodily member   E419.7.

Ghost frightens people (deliberately)   E293.

Ghost of tragic lover haunts scene   E334.2.3.

Ghost rides horse   E581.2.

The Headless Horseman of Braxton County (pp. 89–90)

Headless revenant   E422.1.1.

Actions of headless revenant   E422.1.1.3.

Headless ghost rides a horse   E422.1.1.3.1.

Ghost rides a horse   E581.2.

The Ghost of Sally Robinson (p. 90)

Dress of revenant   E422.4.

Revenant in female dress   E422.4.4.

Revenant in human form   E425.

Revenant as woman   E425.1.

Ghosts walk at certain times   E587.

The Crying Baby (p. 91)

Mysterious ghostlike noises heard   E402.

Ghost cries and screams   E402.1.1.3.

Ghosts walk at certain times   E587.

Ghost in white   E422.4.3.
Revenant in human form   E425.
Revenant as child   E425.3.
Ghost travels swiftly   E599.5.

The Ghost of the Card Player (pp. 91–92)
Ghosts move furniture   E599.6.
Persons who die violent or accidental deaths cannot rest in graves
    E411.10.
Murdered person cannot rest in grave   E413.

An Errant Husband is Disciplined (pp. 92–93)
Ghost visible to one person alone   E421.1.1.
Ghost in white   E422.4.3.

The Walking Ghost (pp. 93–94)
Footsteps of invisible ghost heard   E402.1.2.
Ghost leaves no footprints   E421.2.1.
Invisible ghosts   E421.1.

The Ghost of the Crites Mountain Schoolhouse (pp.94–95)
Mysterious ghostlike noises heard   E402.
Ghost sings   E402.1.1.4.
Ghost in white   E422.4.3.
Revenant in female dress   E422.4.4.
Revenant as lady in white   E425.1.1.
Revenant in human form   E425.
Revenant as woman   E425.1.

The Hidden Treasure of Bear Fork (pp.95–96)
Ghosts protect hidden treasure   E291.
Invisible ghosts   E421.1.
Mysterious ghostlike noises heard   E402.
Vocal sounds of ghost of a human being   E402.1.1.

Wizard Clip (pp. 96–99)
Mysterious ghostlike noises heard   E402.
Spirit slashes clothing   F473.6.2.

Dead without proper funeral rites cannot rest   E412.3.
Invisible ghost   E421.1.
Ghost laid by saying mass   E443.2.1.

WITCHCRAFT, pp. 135–177

Uncle Johnnie Bewitches the Cows (pp. 142–144)
Taboo: Lending to witch   C784.1.
Witch causes animals to behave unnaturally   G265.6.
Curse by disappointed witch   G269.4.
Witch bewitches objects   G265.8.
Witch bewitches household articles   G265.8.1.
Breaking spell by beating the bewitched person or object   G271.4.5.
Witches make cows give bloody milk   D2083.2.1.

Uncle Johnnie Frightens Mrs. Dickens (pp. 144–145)
Witch controls actions of animals   G265.7.
Evil deeds of witches-miscellaneous   G269.
Male witch   G207.

Death and Burial of Uncle Johnnie (pp. 145–146)
Death of witch   G278.
Male witch   G207.

The Black Cat Murders (pp. 146–149)
Witch in animal form   G211.
Witch in form of cat   G211.1.7.
Witch in form of cat has paw cut off, recognized next morning by
    missing hand   G252.
Cat's paw cut; woman's hand missing   D702.1.1.
Murderous witch   G262.
Witch in animal form kills   G262.3.
Witch executed for engaging in witchcraft   G291.
Witches go through keyholes   G249.7.

The Witch of Booger Hole (pp. 149–151)
Witch punishes person who incurs ill will   G269.10.

Death of witch   G278.
Evil deeds of witches   G260.
Witch rides   G241.
Witch rides on person   G241.2.

The Sad Death of Mary Fisher (pp. 151–152)
　　Witch punishes person who incurs her ill will   G269.10.
　　Evil deeds of witches   G260.
　　Illness caused by curse of witch   G263.4.0.1.
　　Witch kills person as punishment   G269.10.1.

The Witch Doctor's Silver Bullet (pp. 153–154)
　　Invisible witch sticks victim with pins   G269.17.
　　Witches go through keyholes   G249.7.
　　Witch punishes person who incurs her ill will   G269.10.
　　Exorcism by injuring image of witch   G271.4.2.
　　Witch overcome or escaped   G270.
　　Silver bullet protects against witch   D1385.4.
　　Rough treatment of object causes injury or death to witch   G275.13.

The Violent Witch (p. 154)
　　Witch punishes person who incurs her ill will   G269.10.
　　Silver bullet protects against witch   D1385.4.
　　Witches go through keyholes   G249.7.
　　Murderous witch   G262.
　　Witch kills person as punishment   G269.10.1.

The Witch of Buck Run (pp. 155–156)
　　Witch bewitches object   G265.8.
　　Witch bewitches household objects   G265.8.1.
　　Witch defeated   G275.
　　Rough treatment of object causes injury or death to witch   G275.13.

The Witchery of Mary Leadum (pp. 156–157)
　　Witch injures, enchants or transforms   G263.
　　Witch's familiar spirit   G225.
　　Other animal as witch's familiar   G225.7.
　　Witch spins   G244.

Murderous witch   G262.

Magic mouse   B183.1.

Witch controls actions of animals   G265.7.

The Mysterious Doe (p. 157)

Witch bewitches gun   G265.8.3.1.

Gun bewitched so that it will not hit target   G265.8.3.1.1.

Witch in the form of an animal is injured or killed as a result of the injury to the animal   G275.12.

Witch in form of a wild beast   G211.2.

Witch in form of a deer   G211.2.4.

Silver bullet protects against witch   D1385.4.

A Witch's Spell is Taken Off (p. 158)

Witch bewitches gun   G265.8.3.1.

Gun bewitched so that it will not hit target   G265.8.3.1.1.

Curse by disappointed witch   G269.4.

Rough treatment of object causes injury or death to witch   G275.13.

The Raccoon Witch (p. 159)

Witch in form of a wild beast   G211.2.

Witch as raccoon   G211.2.8.

Witch bewitches gun   G265.8.3.1.

Gun bewitched so that it will not hit target   G265.8.3.1.1.

Silver bullet protects against witch   D1385.4.

Witch in form of an animal is injured or killed as a result of the injury to the animal   G275.12.

The Witch's Funeral (p. 160)

Witch causes illness of animals   G265.4.2.

Evil deeds of witches   G260.

Marvelous manifestation at death of witch   G278.1.

The Bewitched Pigs (pp. 160–161)

Witch causes animals to behave unnaturally   G265.6.

Witch causes pigs to behave unnaturally   G265.6.1.

Rough treatment of object causes injury or death to witch   G275.13.

The Witch of Bull Run Meets Her Match (pp. 161–162)
Person sells soul to devil in exchange for witch powers   G224.4.
Witch controls actions of animals   G265.7.
Cows magically made dry   D2083.1.
Witch abuses property   G265.
Witch bewitches objects   G265.8.
Object bewitched—miscellaneous   G265.8.4.
Rough treatment of object causes injury or death to witch   G275.13.

The Witch Man of Calhoun County (pp. 162–164)
Object magically raised in air   D2135.0.2.
Object magically moved   D2136.
Person sells soul to devil in exchange for witch powers   G224.4.

The Devil Takes His Victim (pp. 164–167)
Person sells soul to devil in exchange for witch powers   G224.4.
Rough treatment of object causes injury or death to witch   G275.13.
Witch rendered powerless   G273.
Witch causes sickness   G263.4.
Curse by disappointed witch   G269.4.
Witch in form of cat   G211.1.7.
Witches go through keyholes   G249.7.
Witch scratches person   G269.15.
Witch punishes person who incurs her ill will   G269.10.
Exorcism by injuring image of witch   G271.4.2.
Witch hazel used as protection against witches   G272.2.2.
Milk transferred from another's cow by squeezing an axe handle or
   the like   D2083.3.1.

How Witches Got Milk and Butter (pp. 167–168)
Milk transferred from another's cow by magic   D2083.3.

The Milk Witch of Wood County (p. 168)
Milk transferred from another's cow by magic   D2083.3.
Witch transfers milk from another's cow to a vessel   D2083.3.3.
Milk transferred from another's cow by squeezing an axe handle or
   the like   D2083.3.1.

The Gilmer County Witch Plays a Trick (pp. 168–169)
   Milk transferred from another's cow by squeezing an axe handle or
      the like   D2083.3.1.
   Witch punishes person who incurs her ill will   G269.10.

The Black is Beaten (pp. 169–170)
   Witch punishes person who incurs her ill will   G269.10.
   Witch in animal form   G211.
   Witch in form of a cat   G211.1.7.
   Witch in form of an animal is injured or killed as a result of the injury to
      the animal   G275.12.

Another Way to Break a Spell (p. 170)
   Curse by disappointed witch   G269.4.
   Breaking spell by beating the person or object bewitched   G271.4.5.

How to Kill a Witch (p. 171)
   Exorcism by injuring image of witch   G271.4.2.
   Rough treatment of object causes injury or death to witch   G275.13.

White Bear (pp. 171–174)
   Witch transforms person to animal   G263.1.
   Witch transforms man to bear   G263.1.1.
   Witch bewitches clothing   G265.8.2.
   Bride test: domestic skill   H383.

A Young Man Fixes the Witch of Bull Run (pp. 174–175)
   Rough treatment of object causes injury or death to witch   G275.13.
   Witch punishes person who incurs her ill will   G269.10.
   Curse by disappointed witch   G269.4.

Recollections of Witchcraft (pp. 175–177)
   Exorcism by injuring image of witch   G271.4.2.
   Breaking spell by beating person or object bewitched   G271.4.5.
   Witch hazel used for protection against witches   G272.2.2.
   Witch causes pigs to act unnaturally   G265.6.1.